MANDALA
Coloring Book for Adults

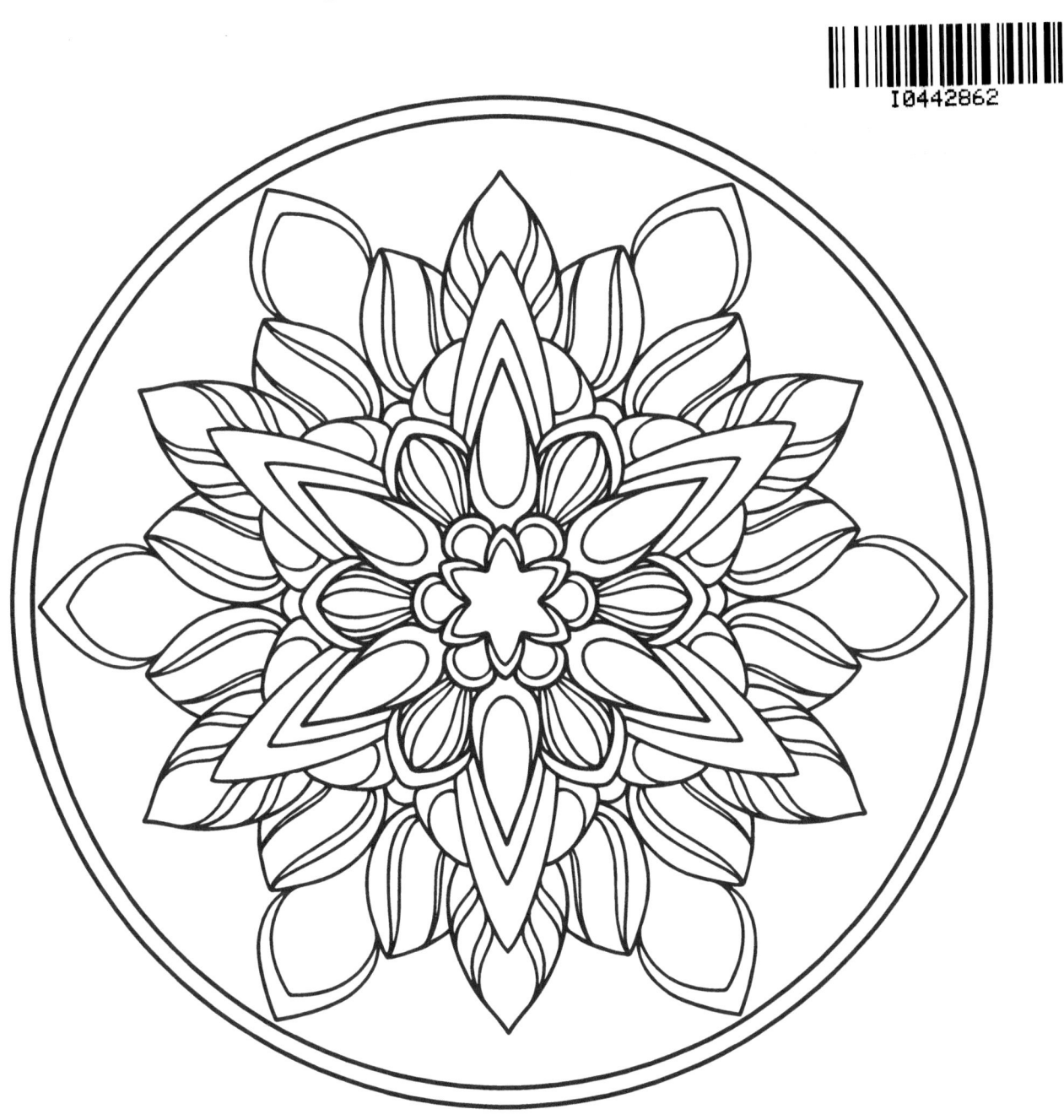

Vanessa Bentley

www.vanessabentley.com

60 Intricate Mandalas for you to color. There are some easy ones, but most are complex enough to keep your mind off all your worries for several hours.

A variety of materials can be used to color these images, from color pencils to markers. **To prevent bleed-through when coloring, place a blank sheet of paper or card stock between the pages.**

Images have been printed on one side of the page only.

All images in this book are original drawings and designs by Vanessa Bentley.

Visit www.vanessabentley.com

Sign up for my newsletter

Subscribers get:

- Free coloring pages to download
- News of upcoming releases
- Giveaways and contests

You can also follow me on

- @vanessabentleyart
- @artbyvanessa

Copyright © Vanessa Bentley 2020

All rights reserved. No part of this publication may be reproduced, distributed, or transmitted in any form or by any means, including photocopying, recording, or other electronic or mechanical methods, without the prior written, dated and signed permission of the copyright owner.

Thank you for purchasing this book. I hope that you found the illustrations fun and interesting to color in.

If you enjoyed the book then I would be incredibly grateful if you would share your experience by either rating or leaving a few words in the review section where you purchased this book online.

Your feedback is important and helps me to continue creating work like this.

Vanessa Bentley

Also by Vanessa Bentley

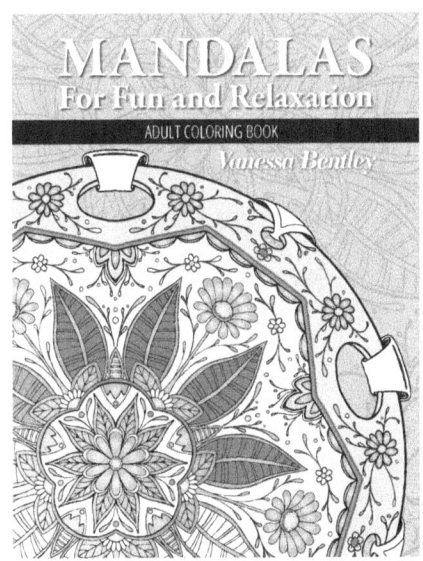 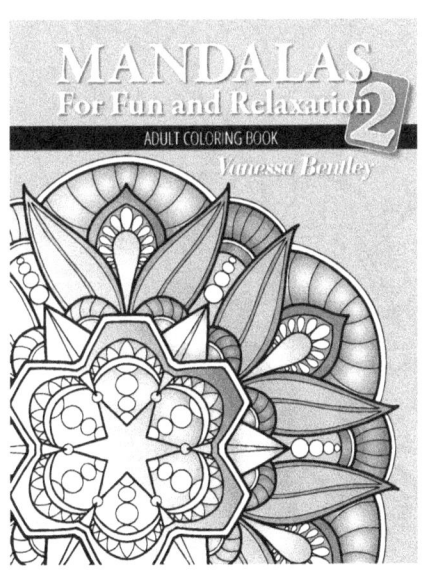 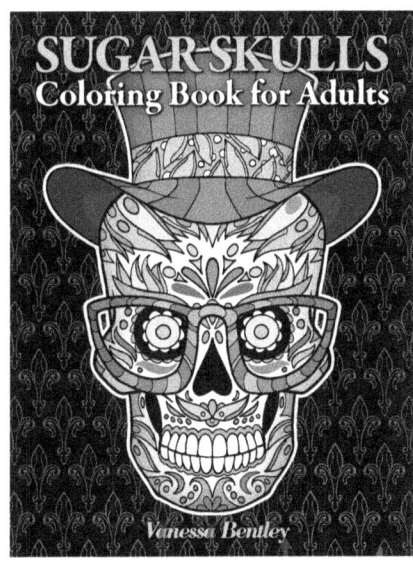

MANDALAS
For Fun and Relaxation

MANDALAS
For Fun and Relaxation 2

SUGAR SKULLS
Coloring Book for Adults

Mandalas

"Mandala" is a Sanskrit word that means "circle"

Mandalas have been around for centuries and it has been discovered that drawing or coloring mandalas is relaxing and uplifting. Mandala patterns are repeated around a centre point. Some designs are basic and simple while others can be very detailed and complex.

Although Mandalas mostly consist of abstract shapes, modern Mandalas can consist of animals, flowers and even figures or faces.

Some Mandalas in this book may be very simple. You can color them as they are, but if you are feeling adventurous you can always take a pen and add your own touches to the mandala.

The Benefits of Coloring

Not everyone can draw or paint, that is where coloring books are great. The artist creates the image and puts it out there for someone else to complete the work by adding color in the medium of their choice. Many coloring book artists are pleasantly surprised when they get to see how colorists bring their images to life. So the artist and colorist are now in fact collaborators in the project.

Participating in a creativity such as coloring in occupies the part of the brain that deals with stress and worry. How? Well, when you color in you have to decide what you are going to color, what medium to use, what color or color combinations you are going to use and how you are going to color it.

Many retirement homes have started giving coloring pages to their residents to color in. It is not only good for hand eye coordination, but it is uplifting, relaxing and gives people a sense of accomplishment.

How to Color in

I believe that you should go with what you feel. Practice makes perfect and as you color more and more, you will get to know which colors you like putting together. If you are worried that you will mess up your image, you may make a copy of the page and practice on that copy.

Use the page provided to test your art materials and color combinations

If you want to learn more about coloring techniques, there are many tutorials on YouTube that will help you advance as a colorist.

Happy coloring!

You can use this page to test your art materials

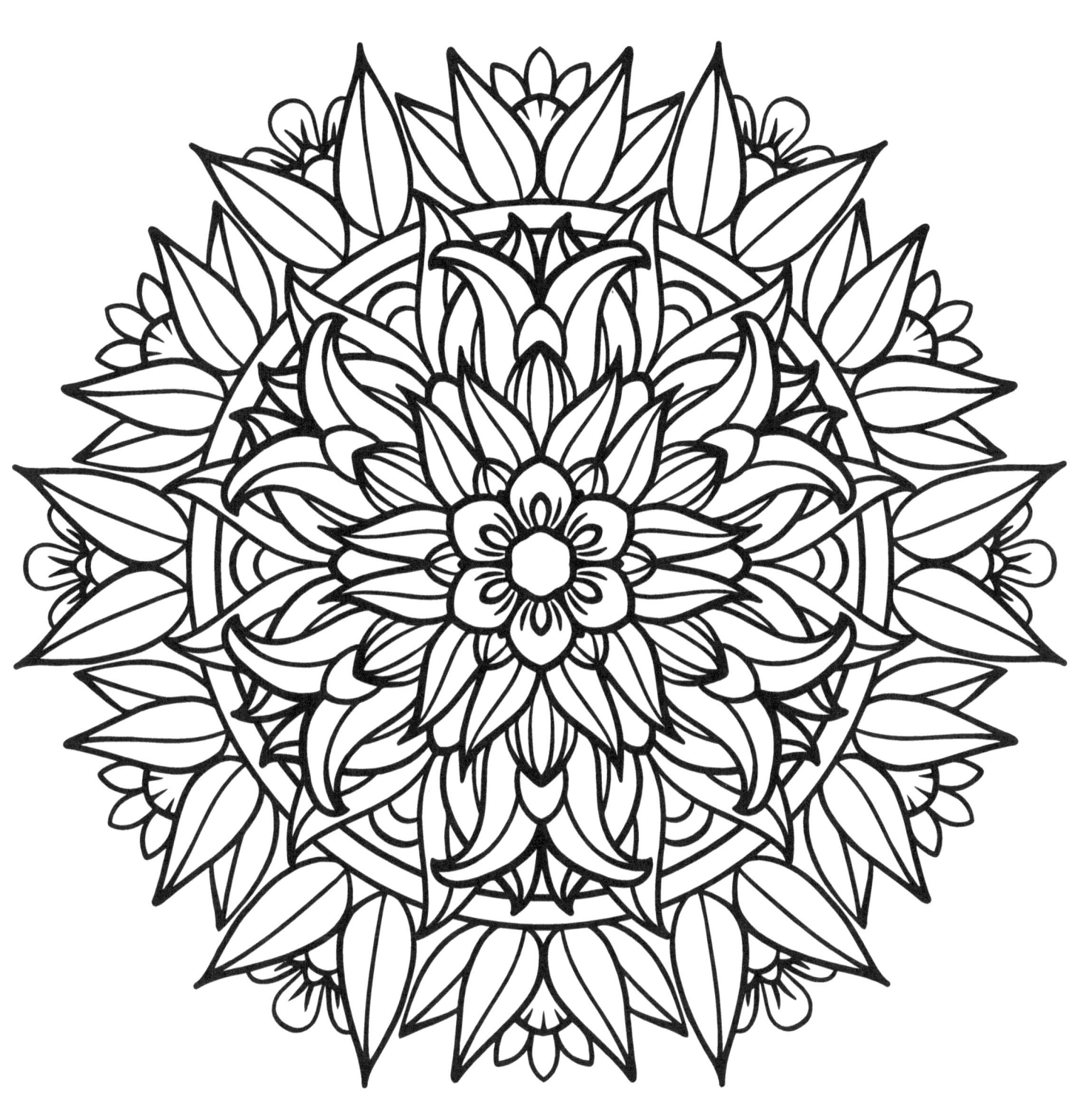

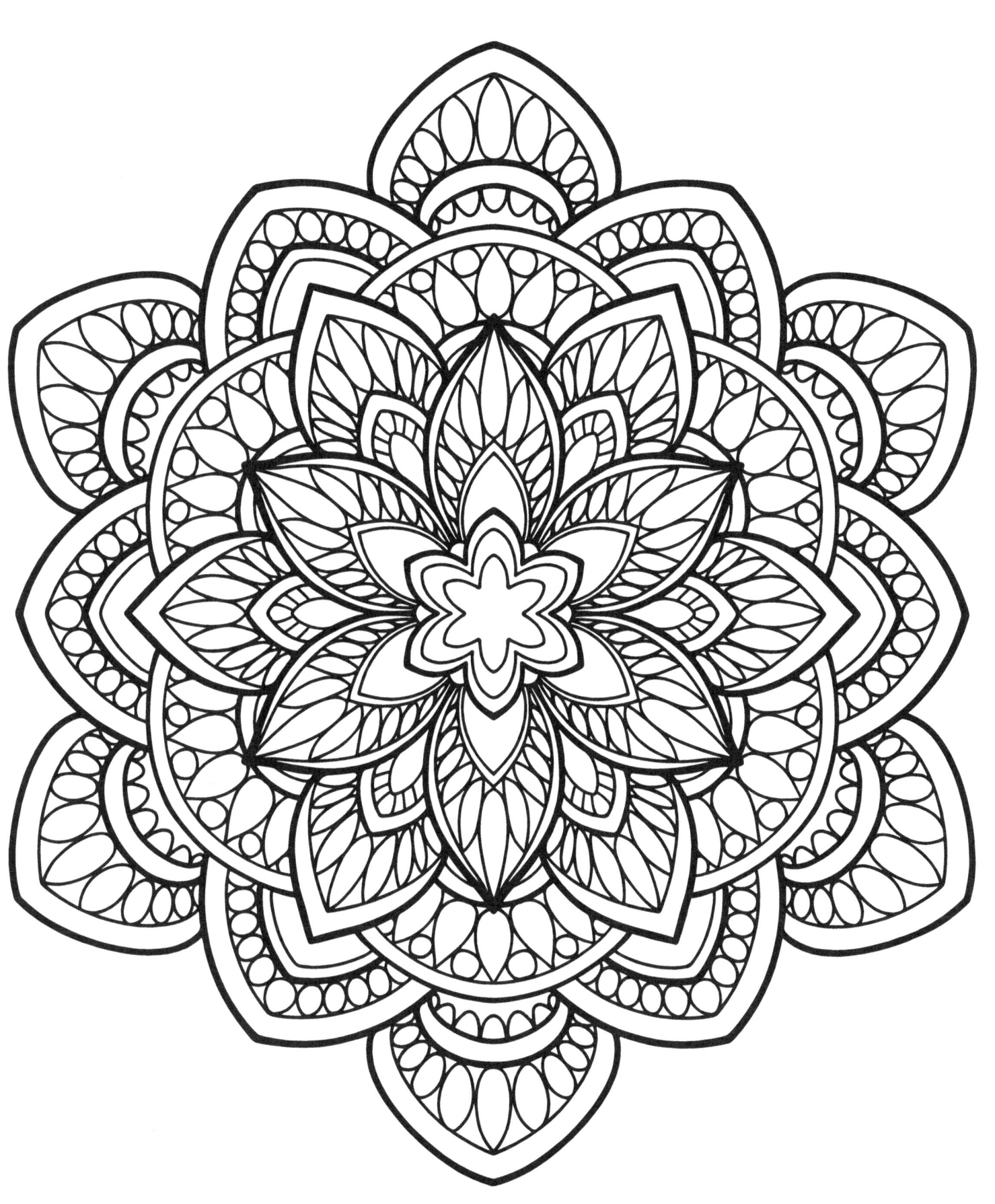

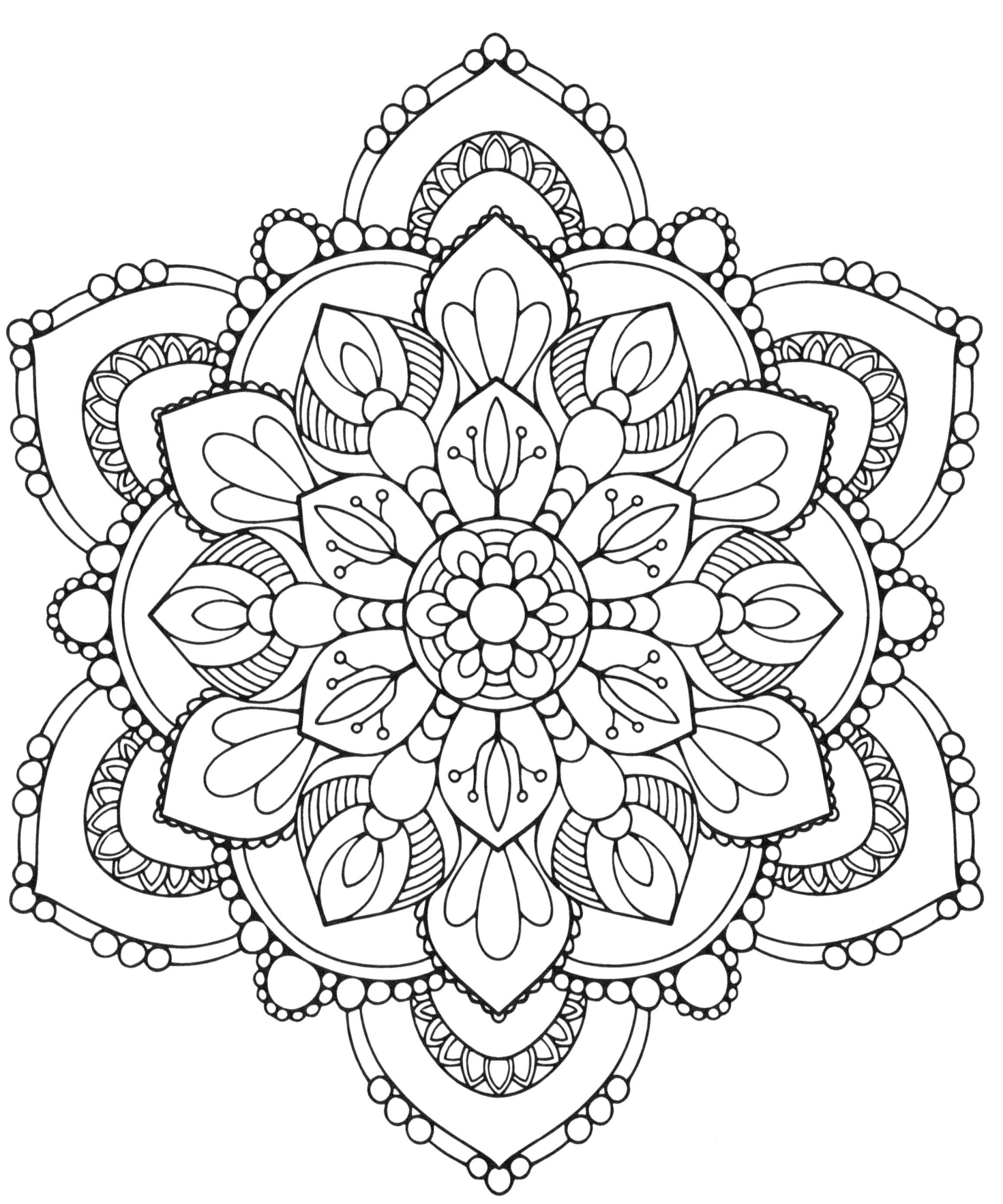

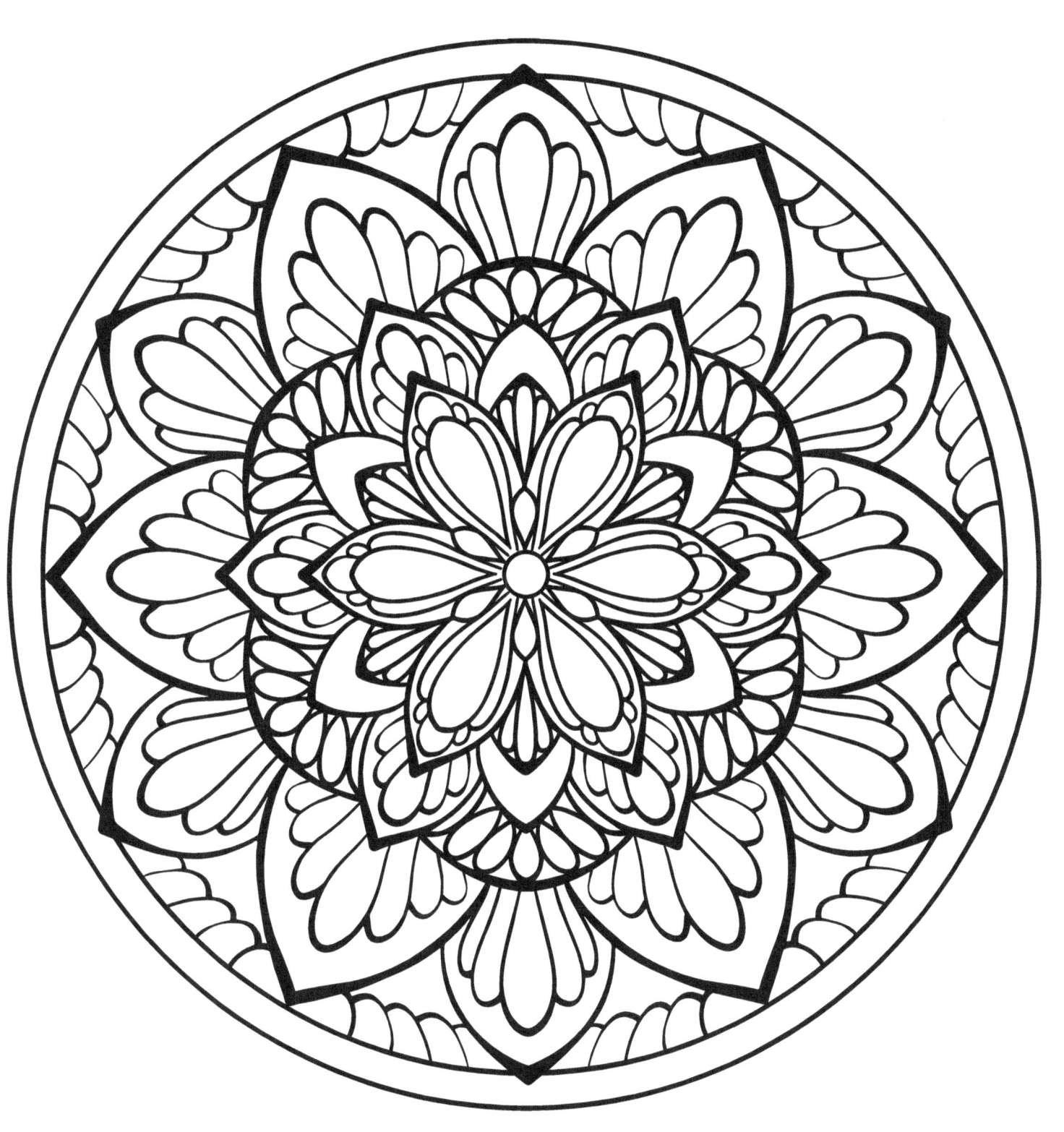

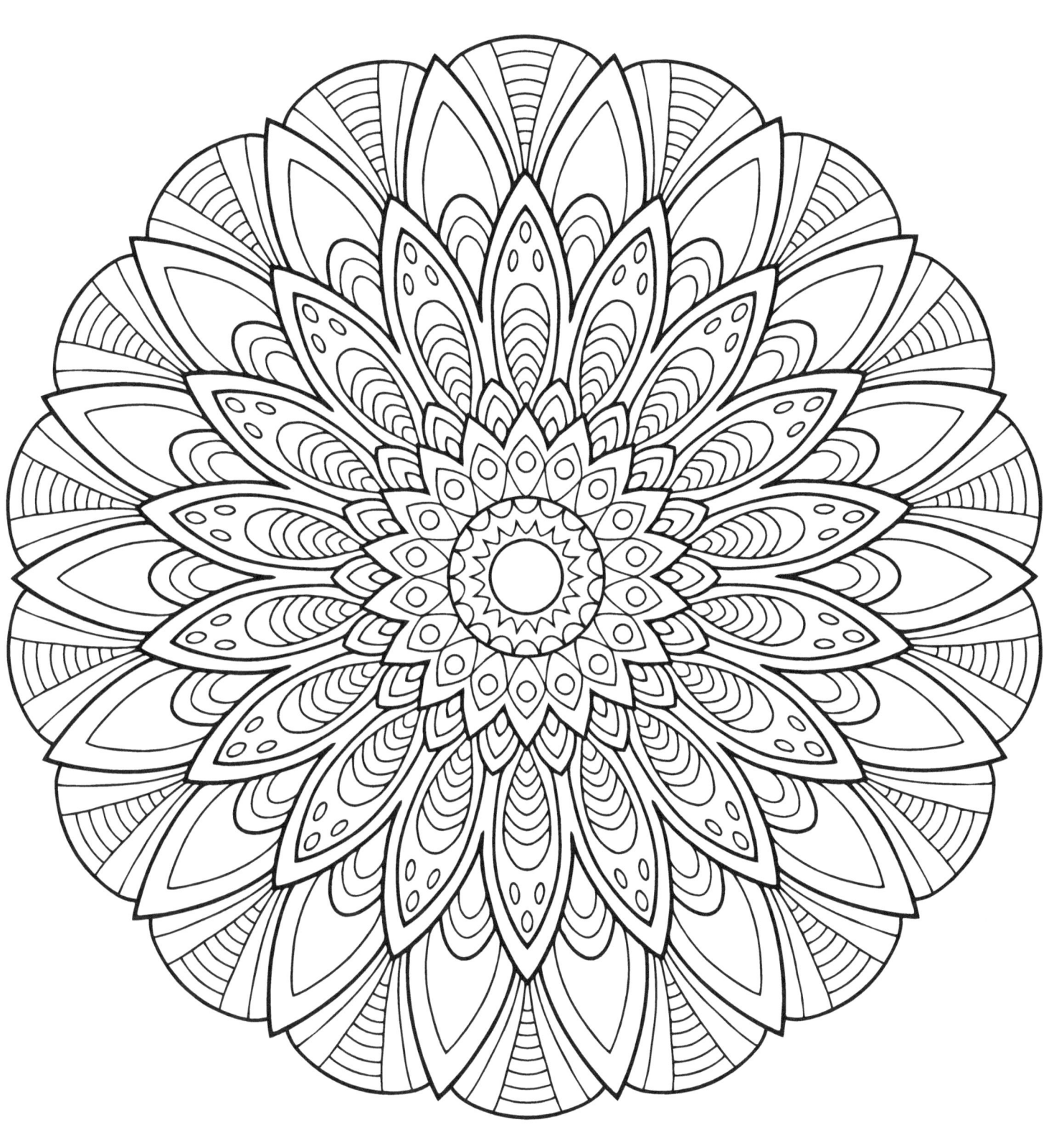

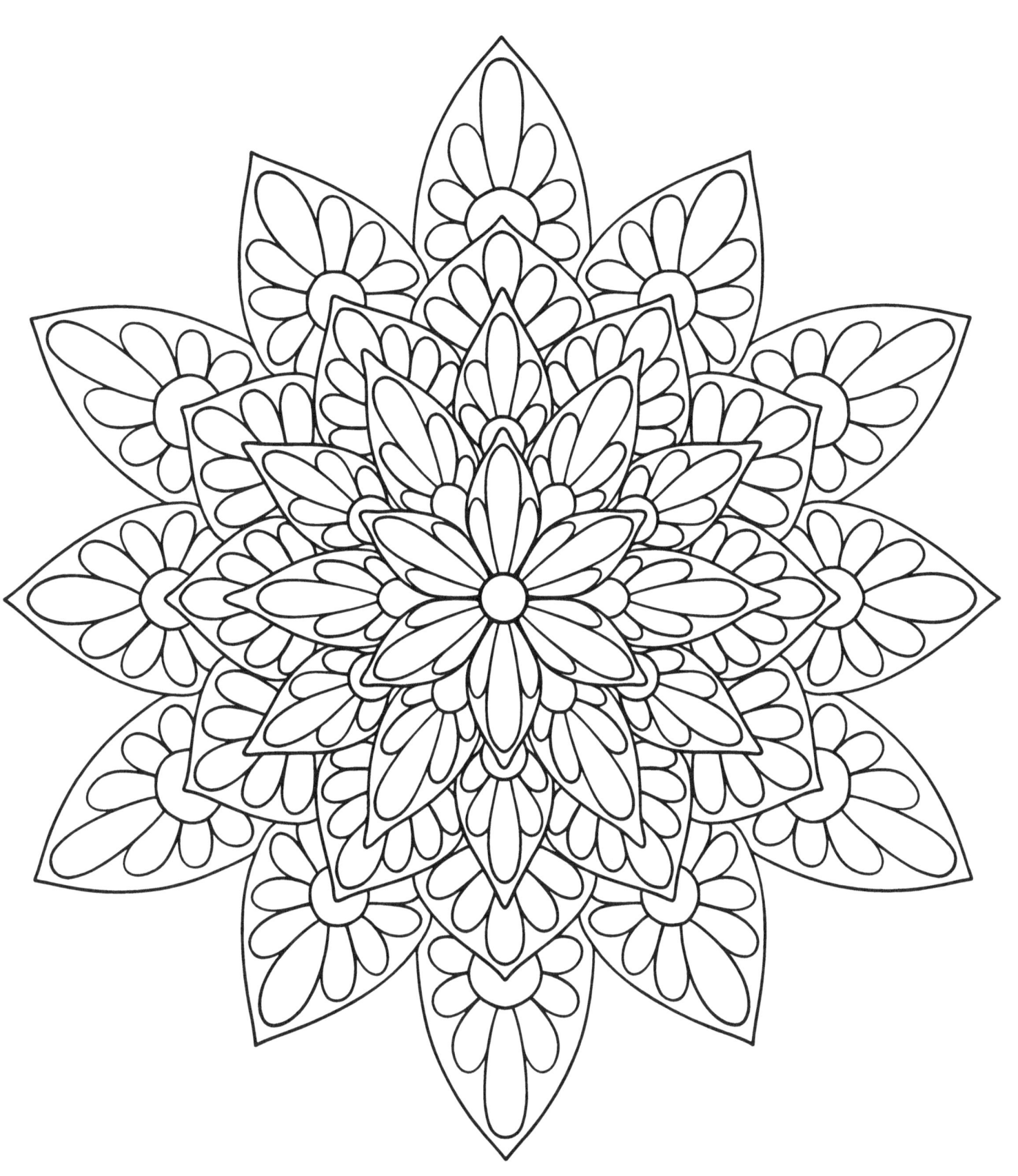

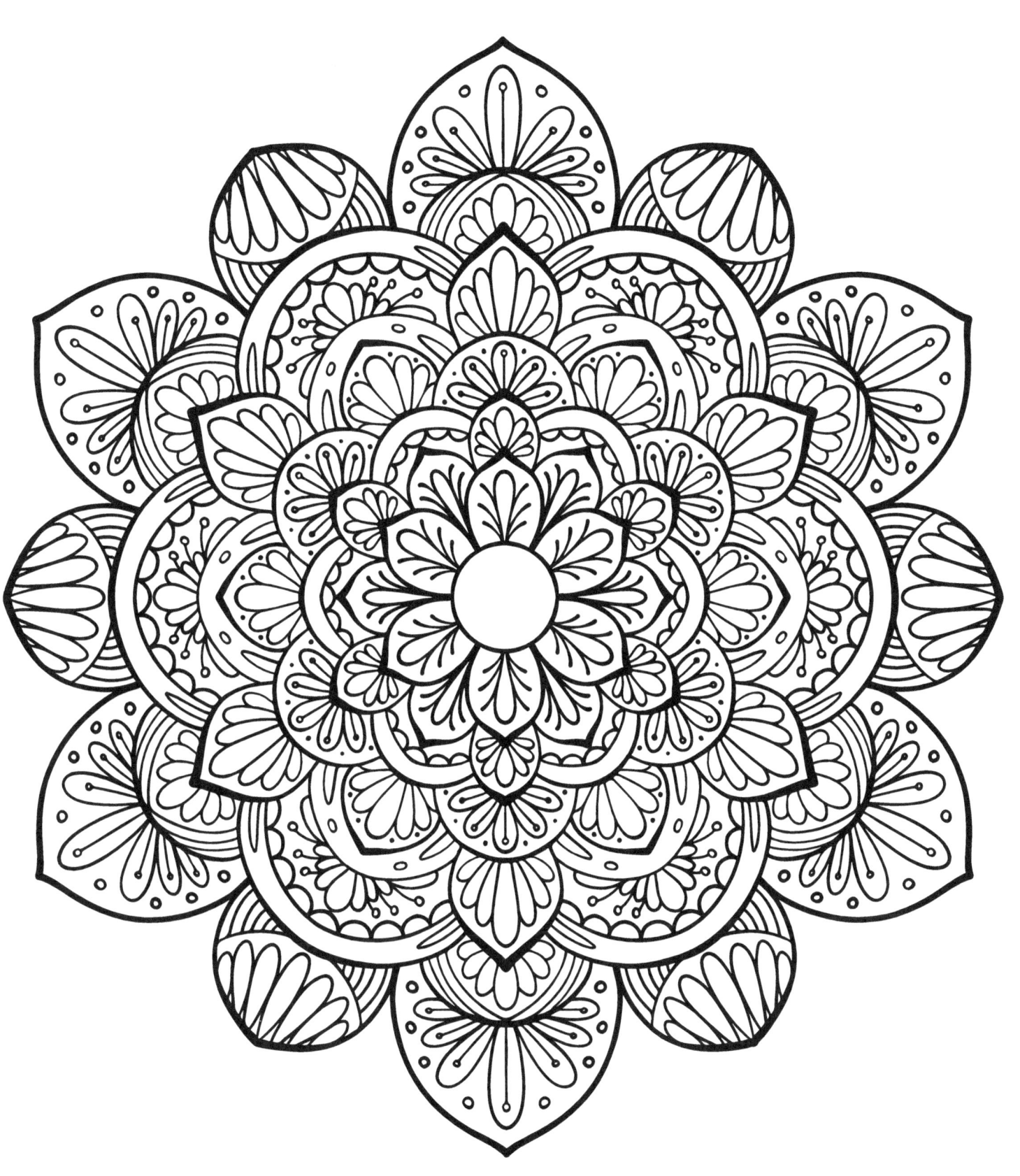

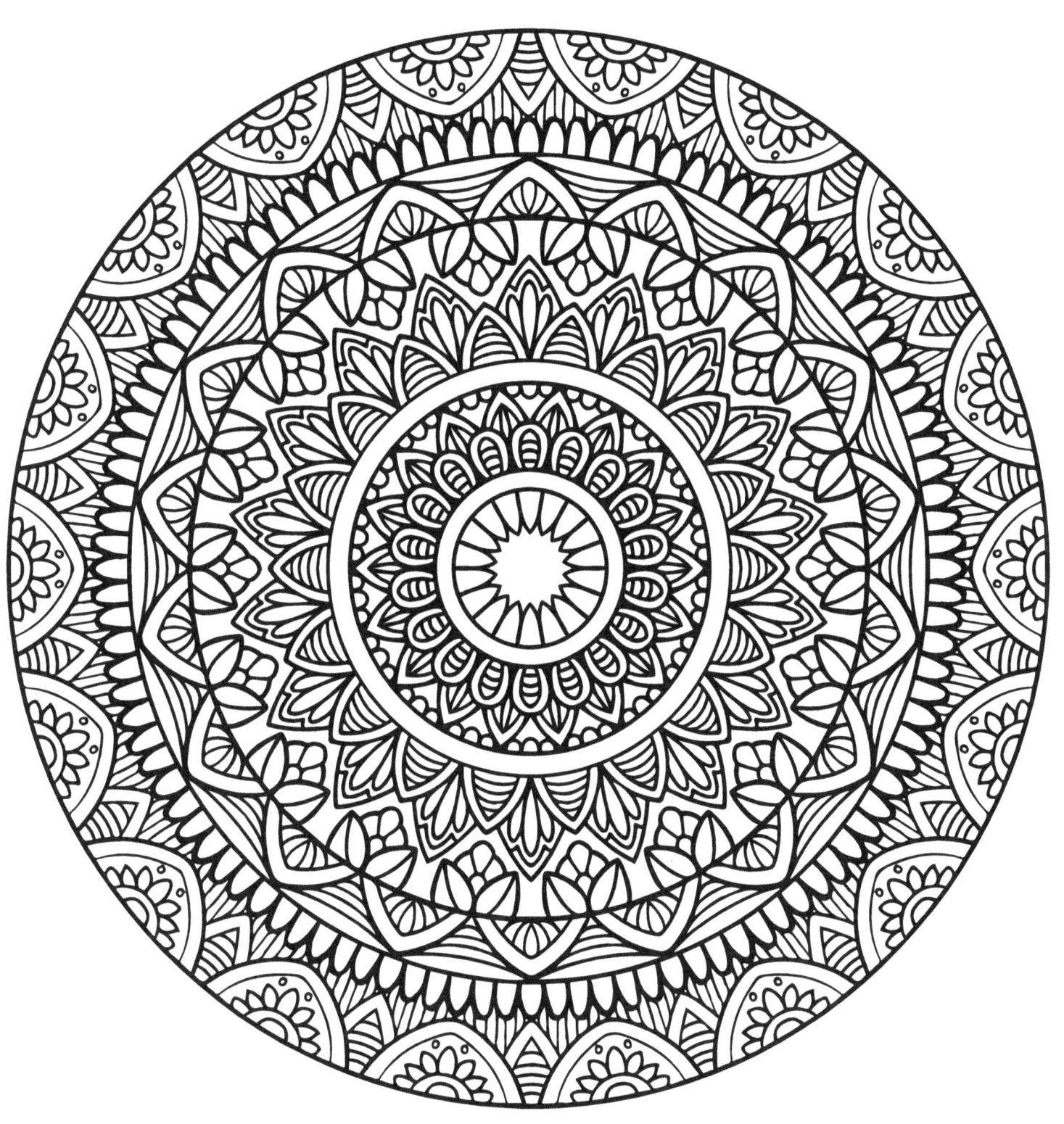

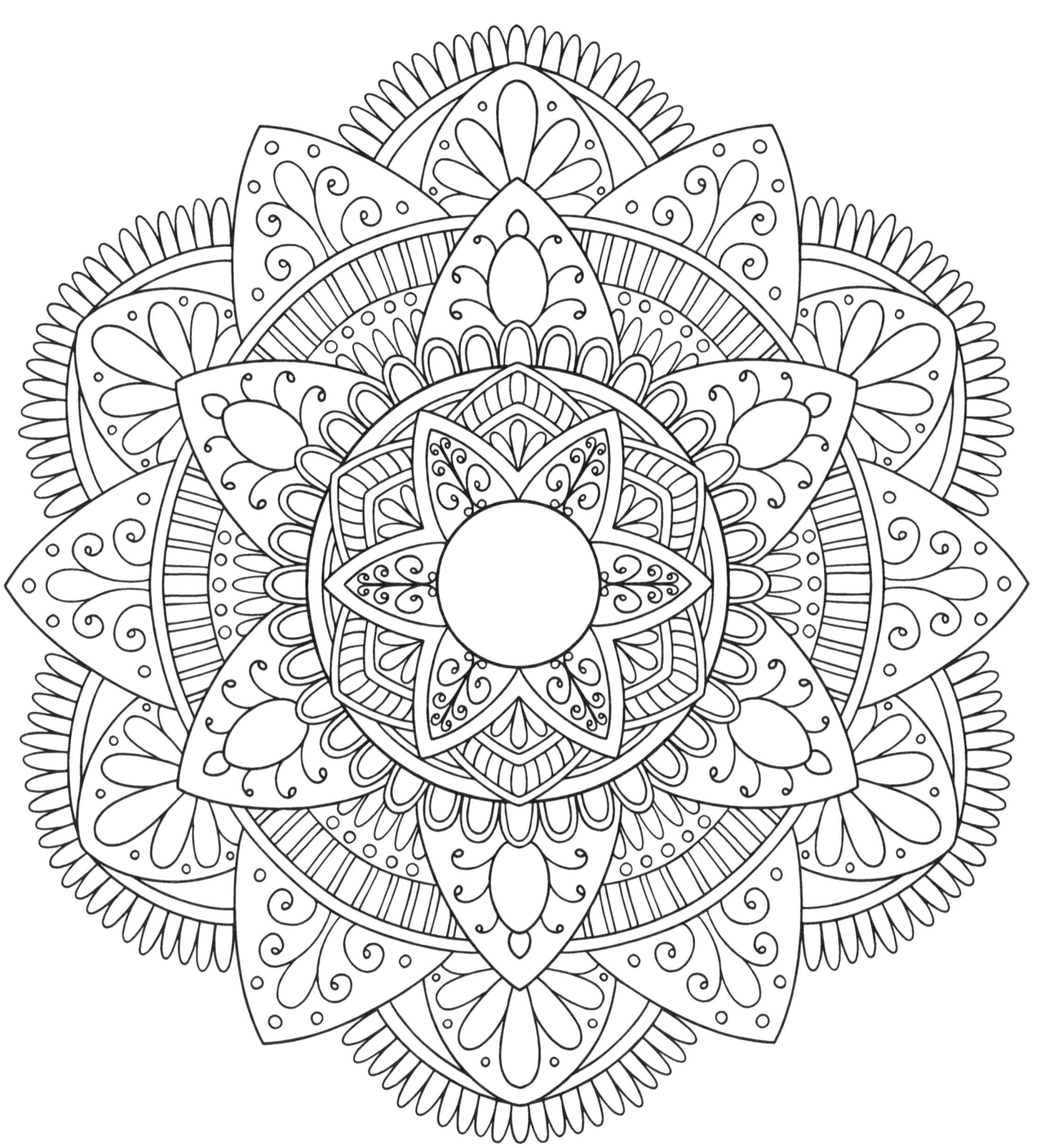

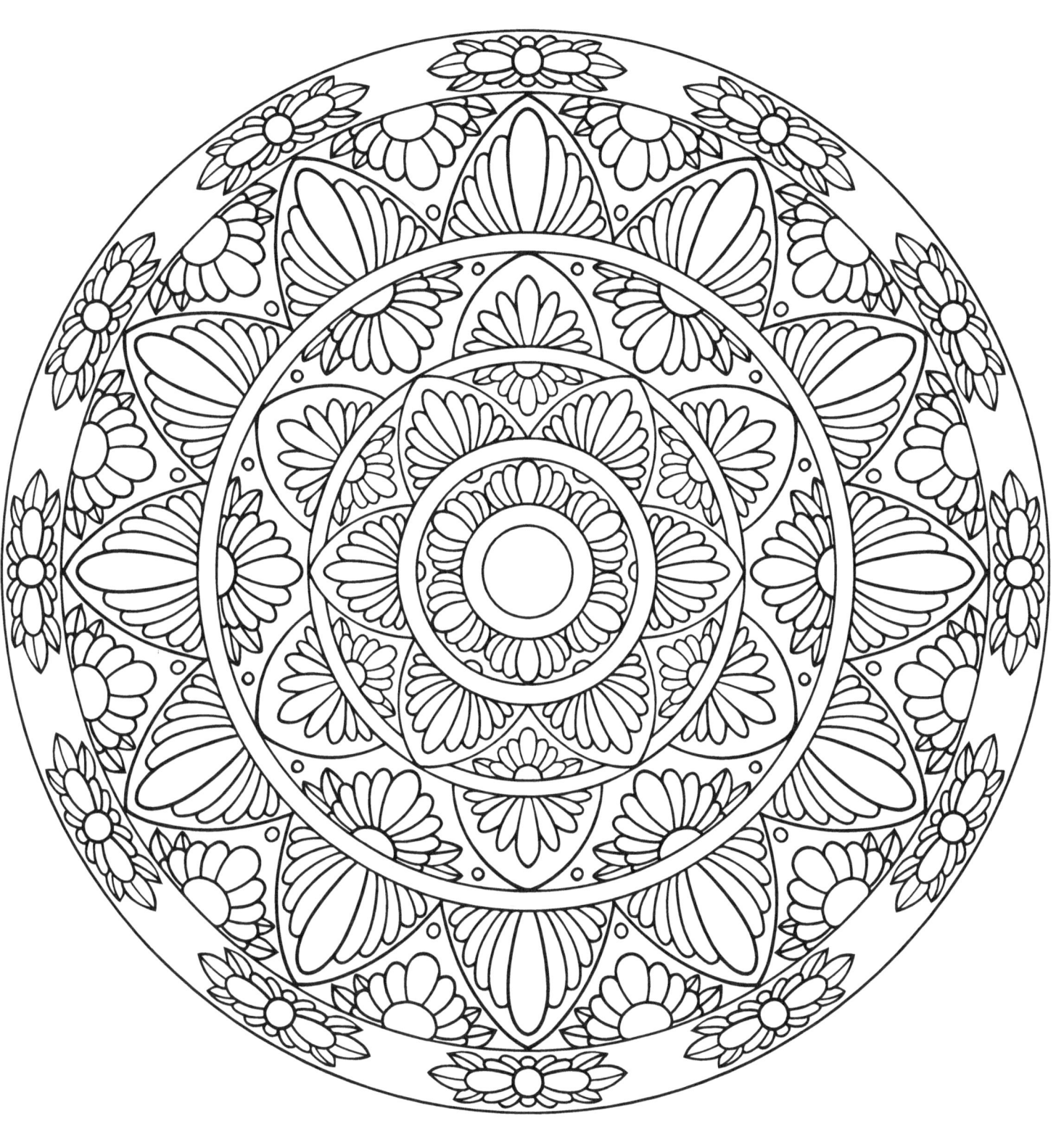

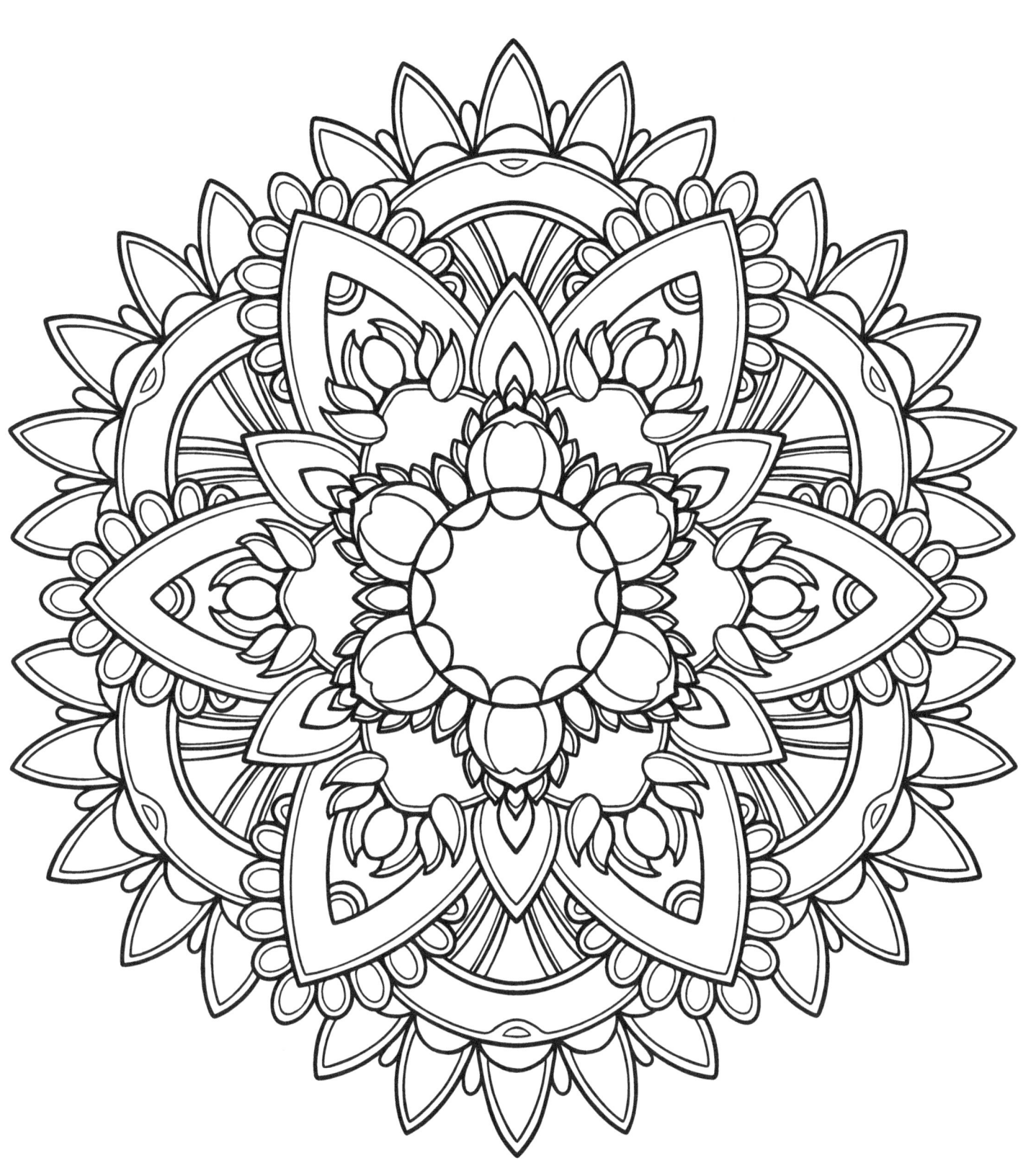

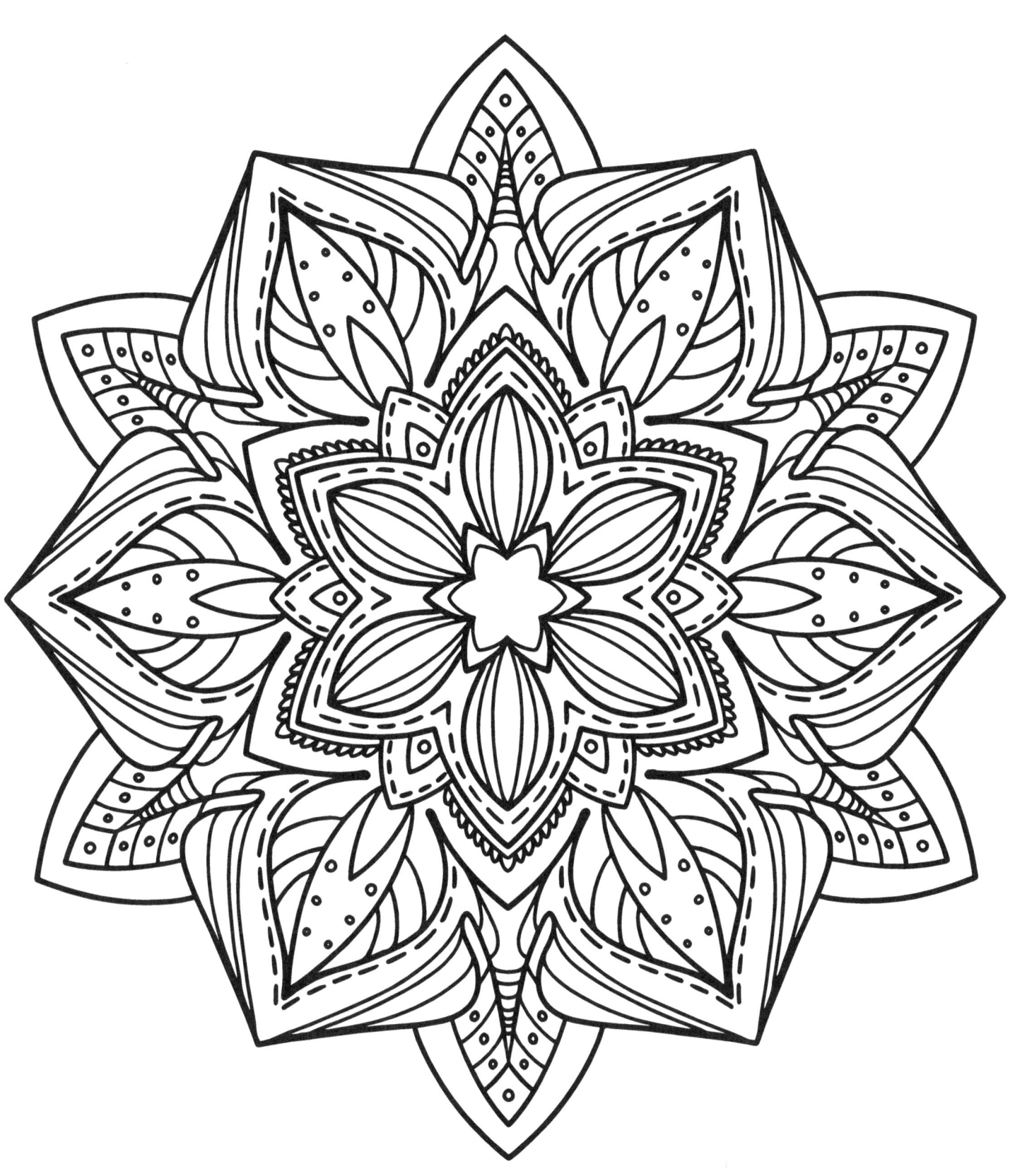

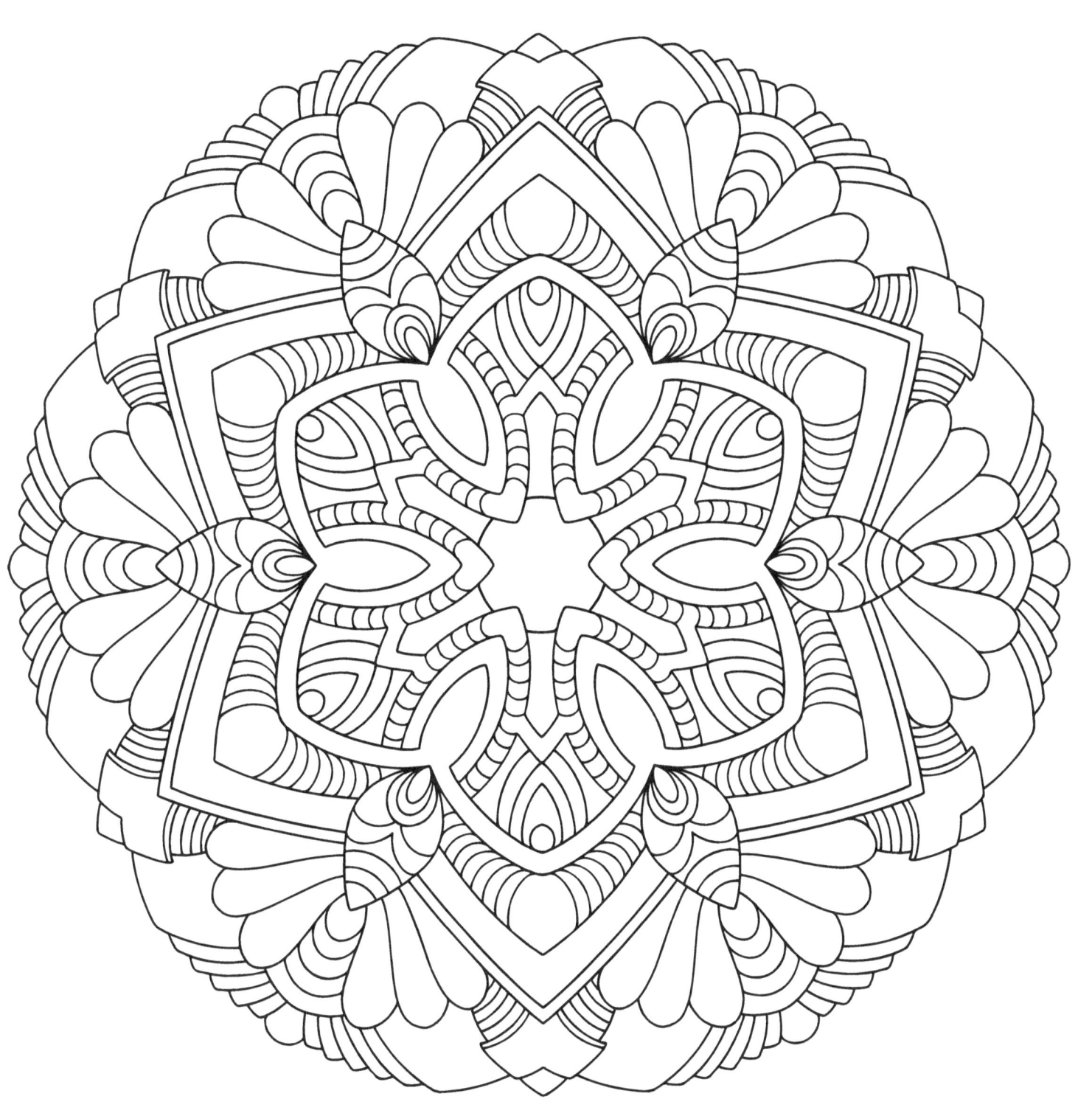

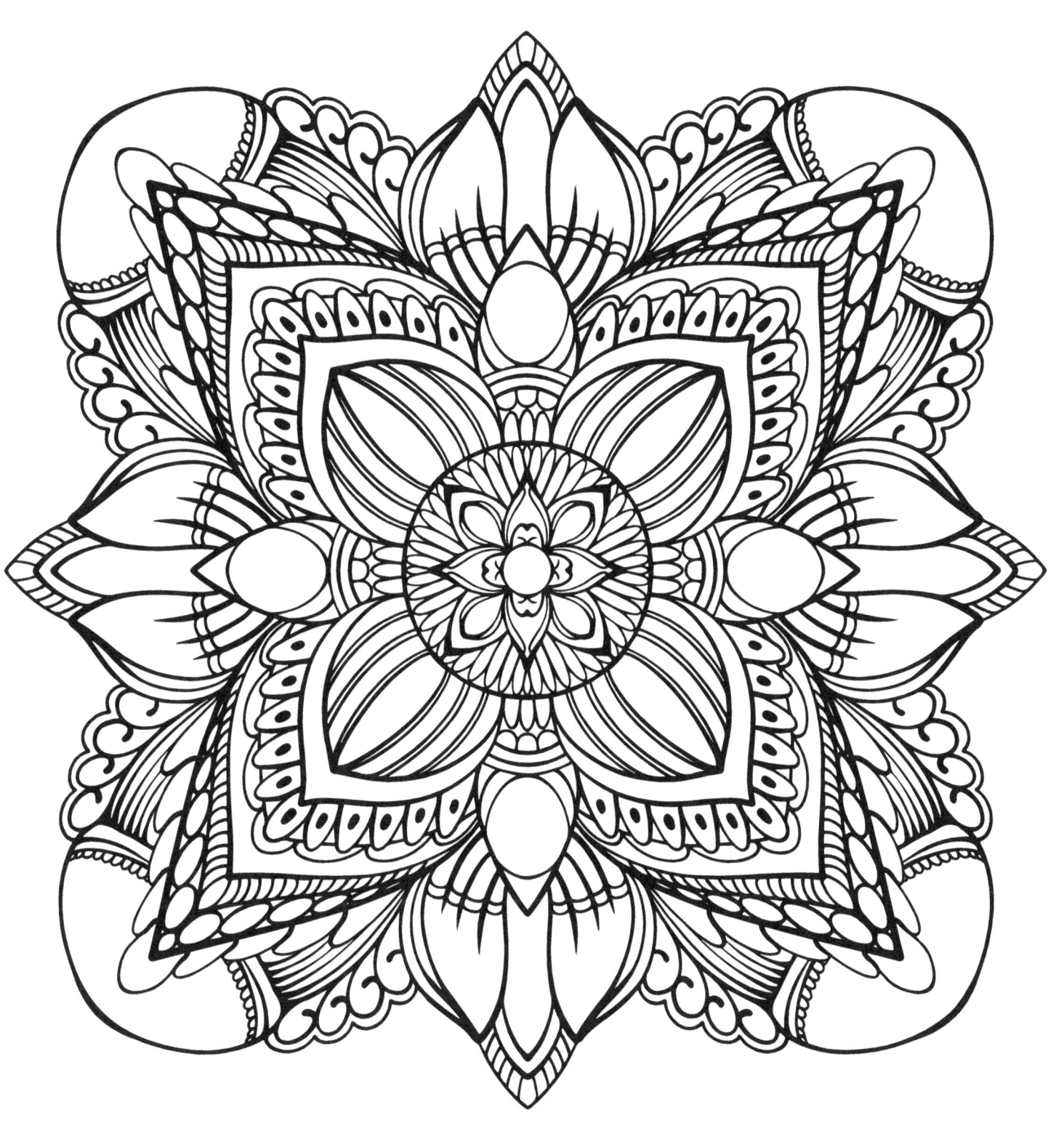

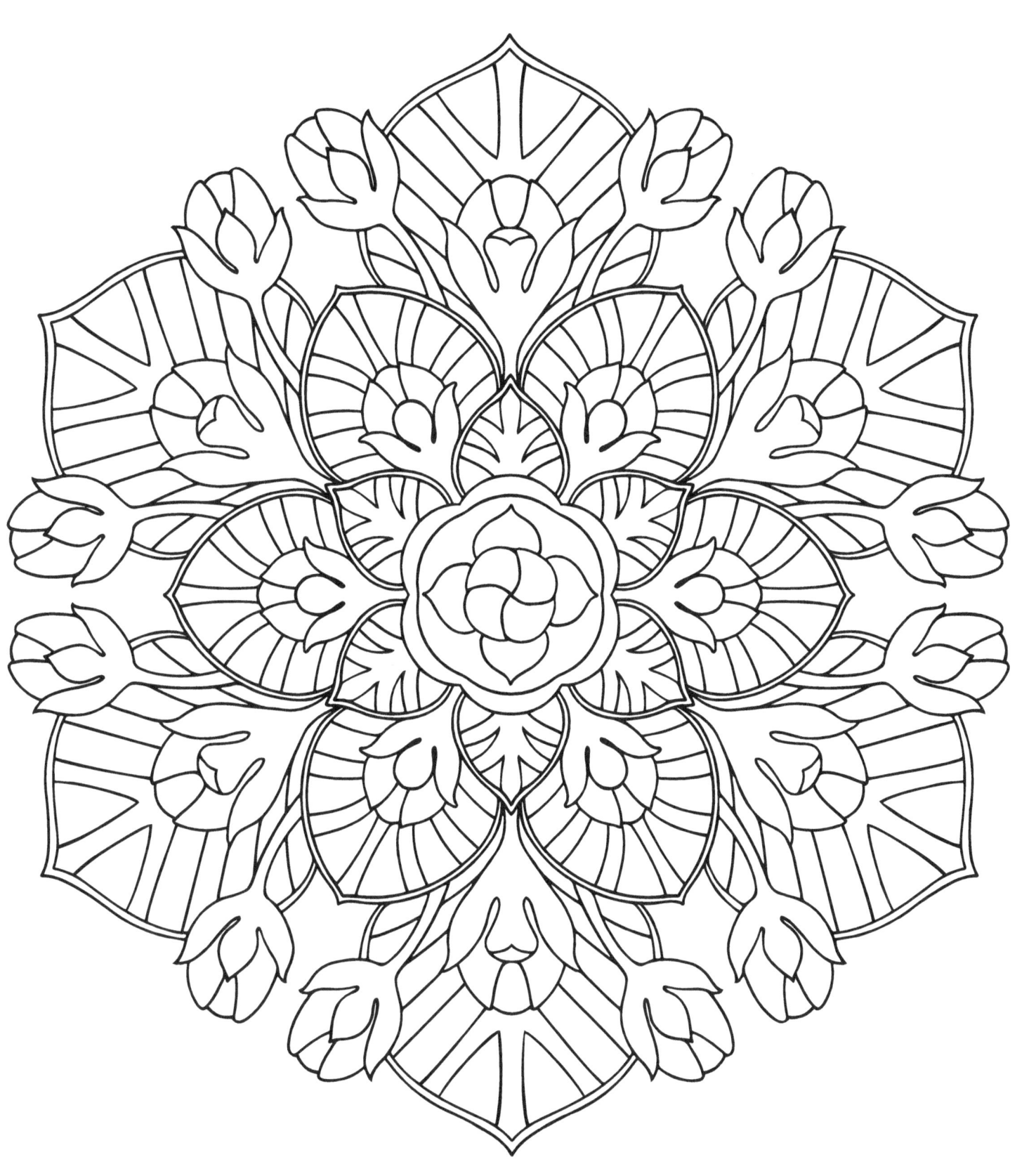

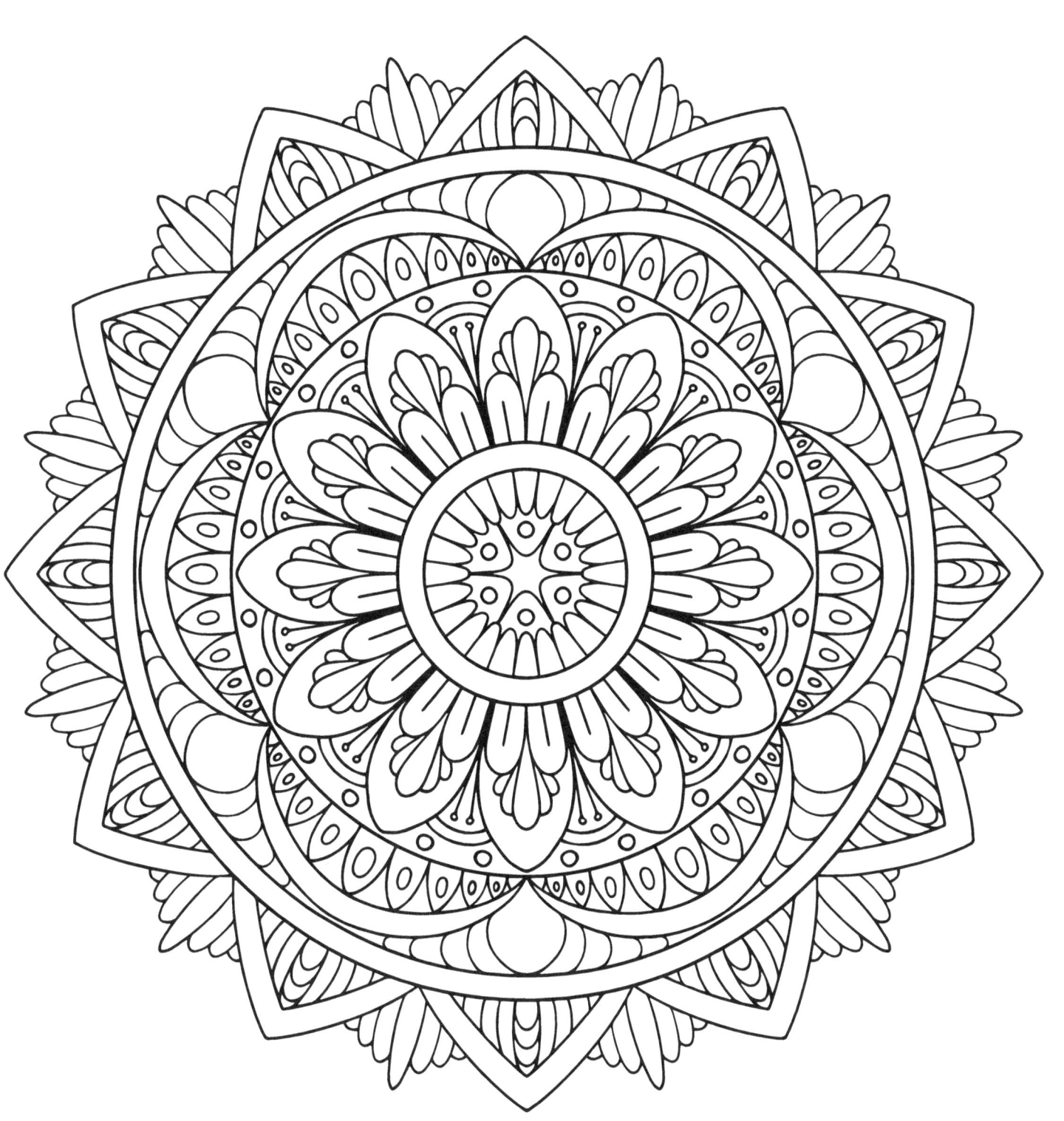

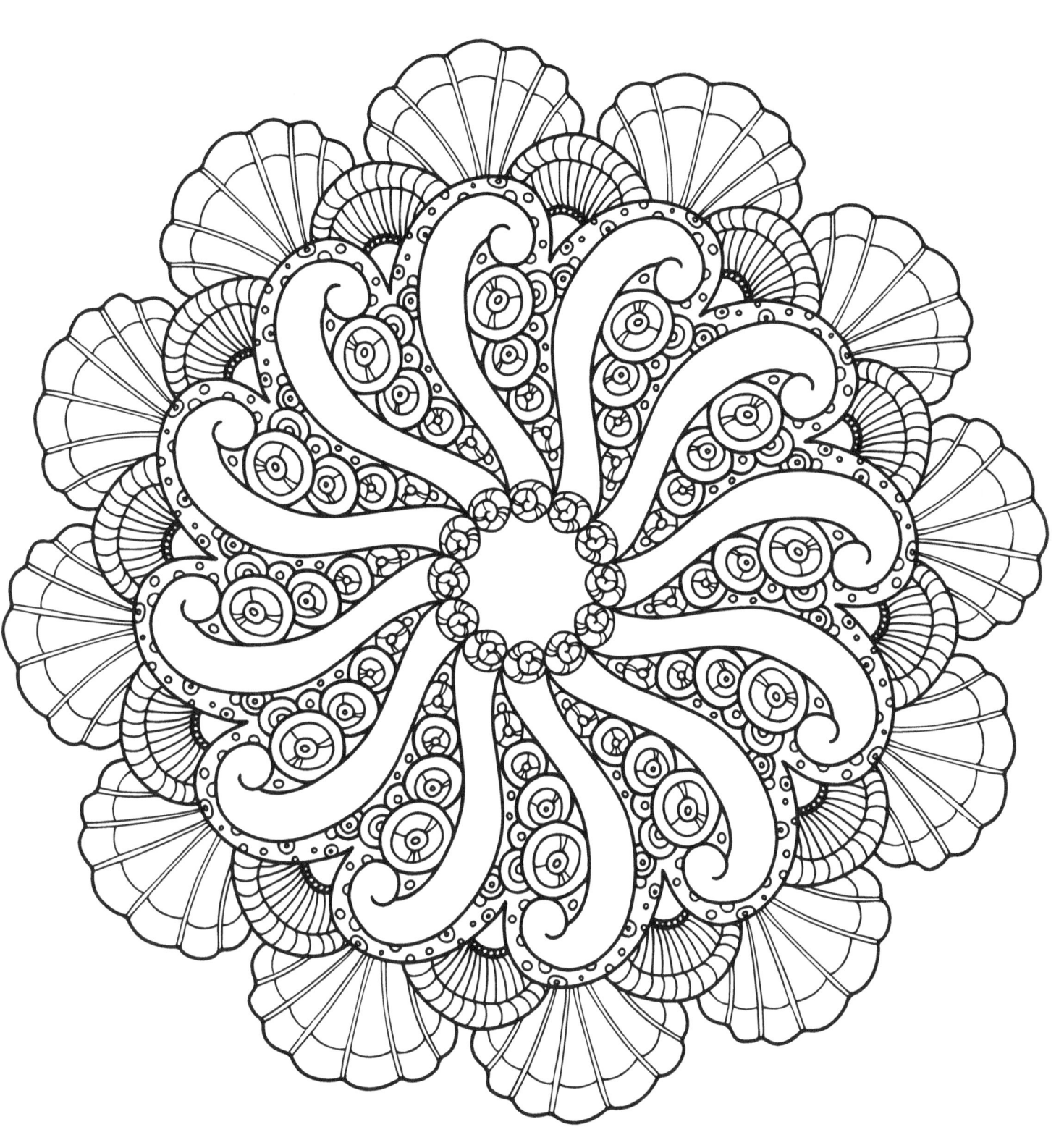

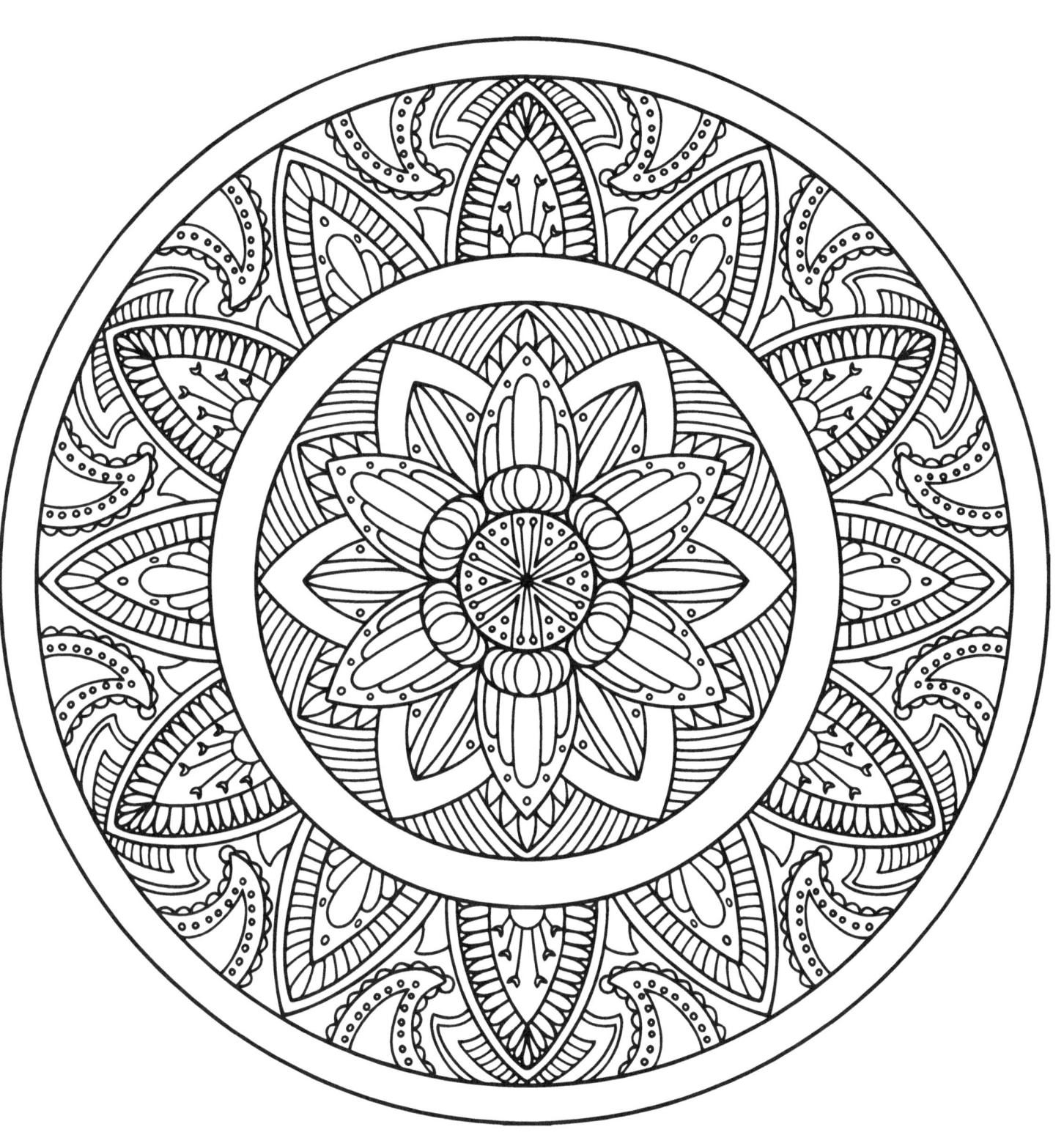

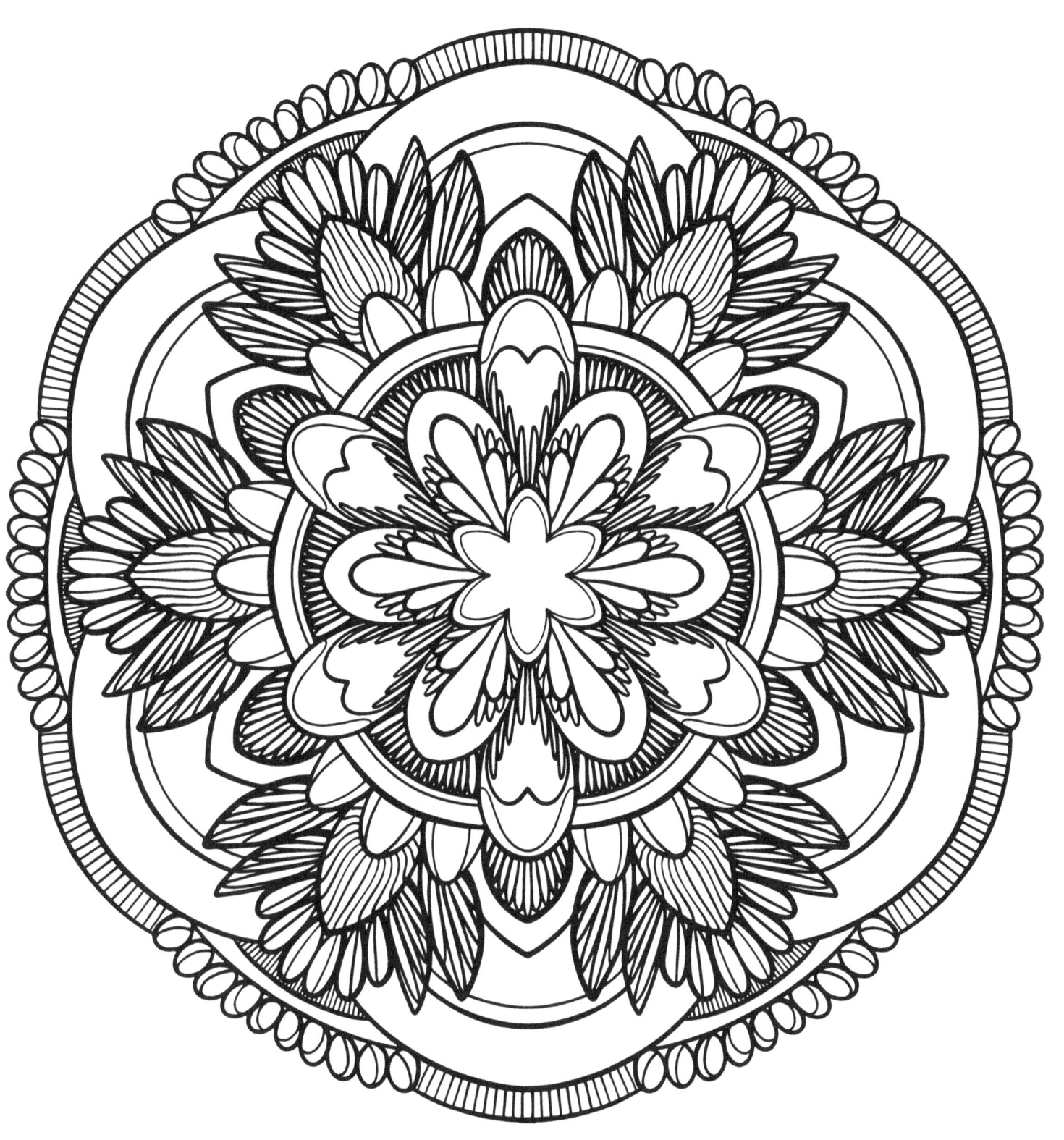

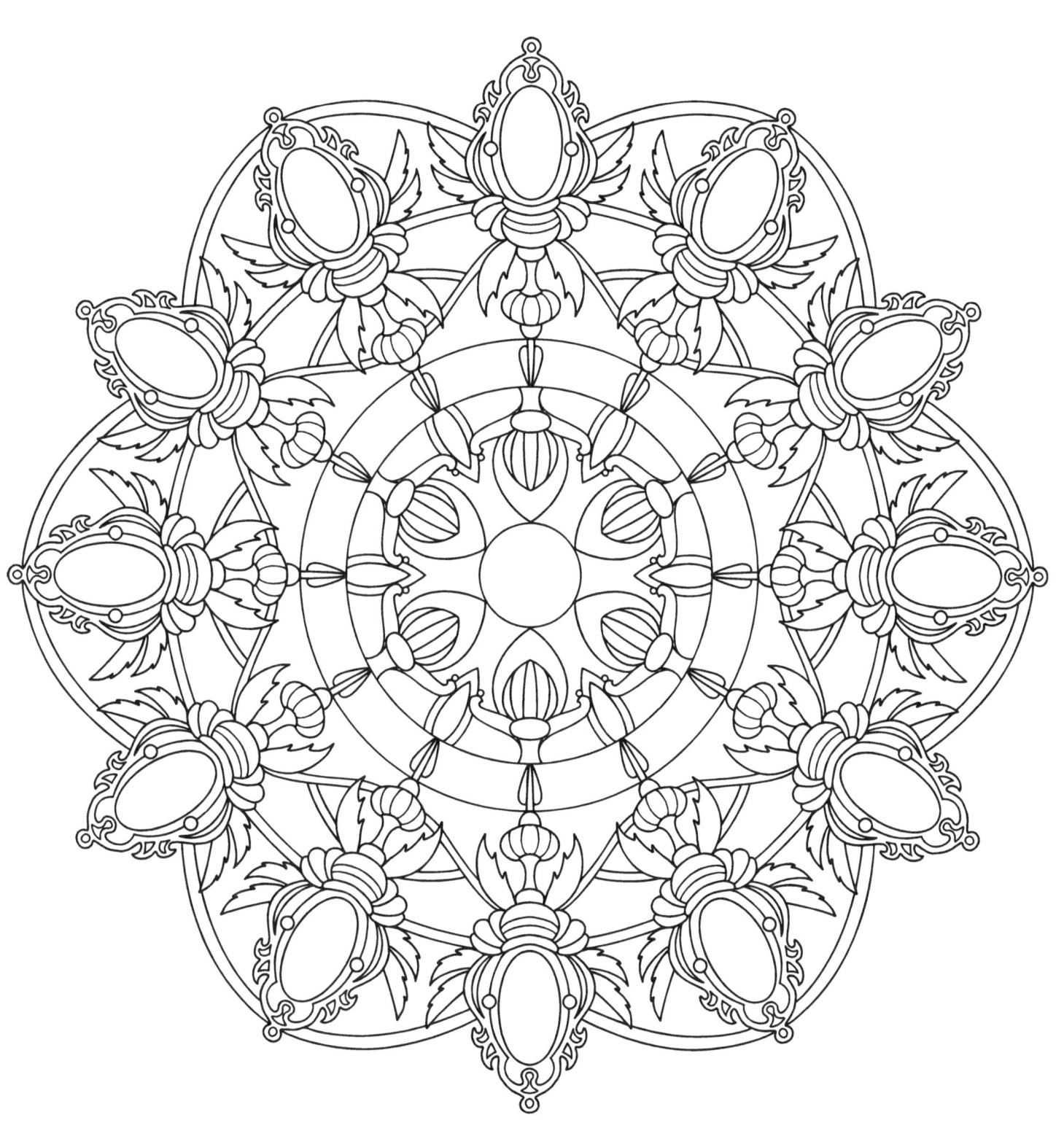

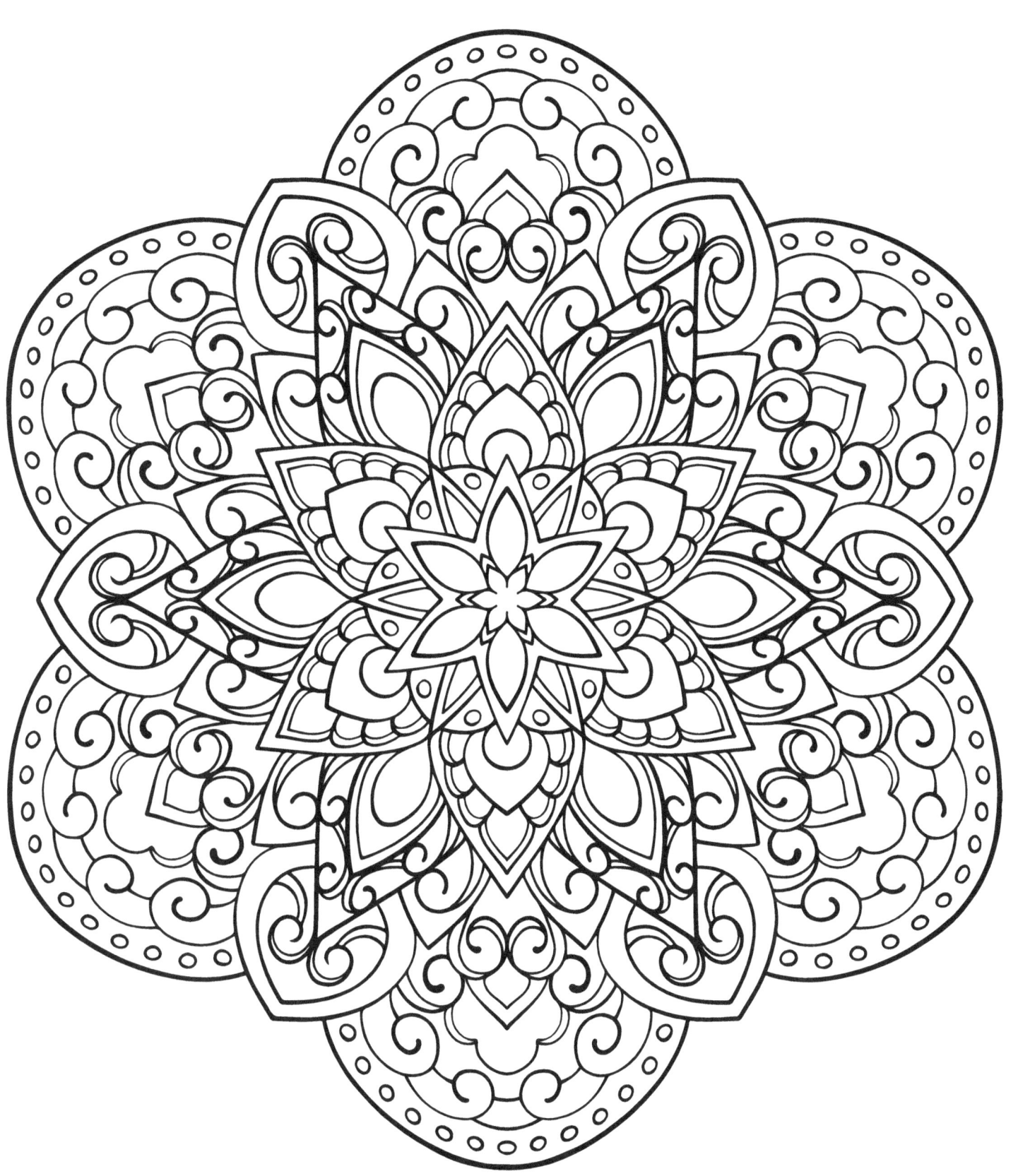

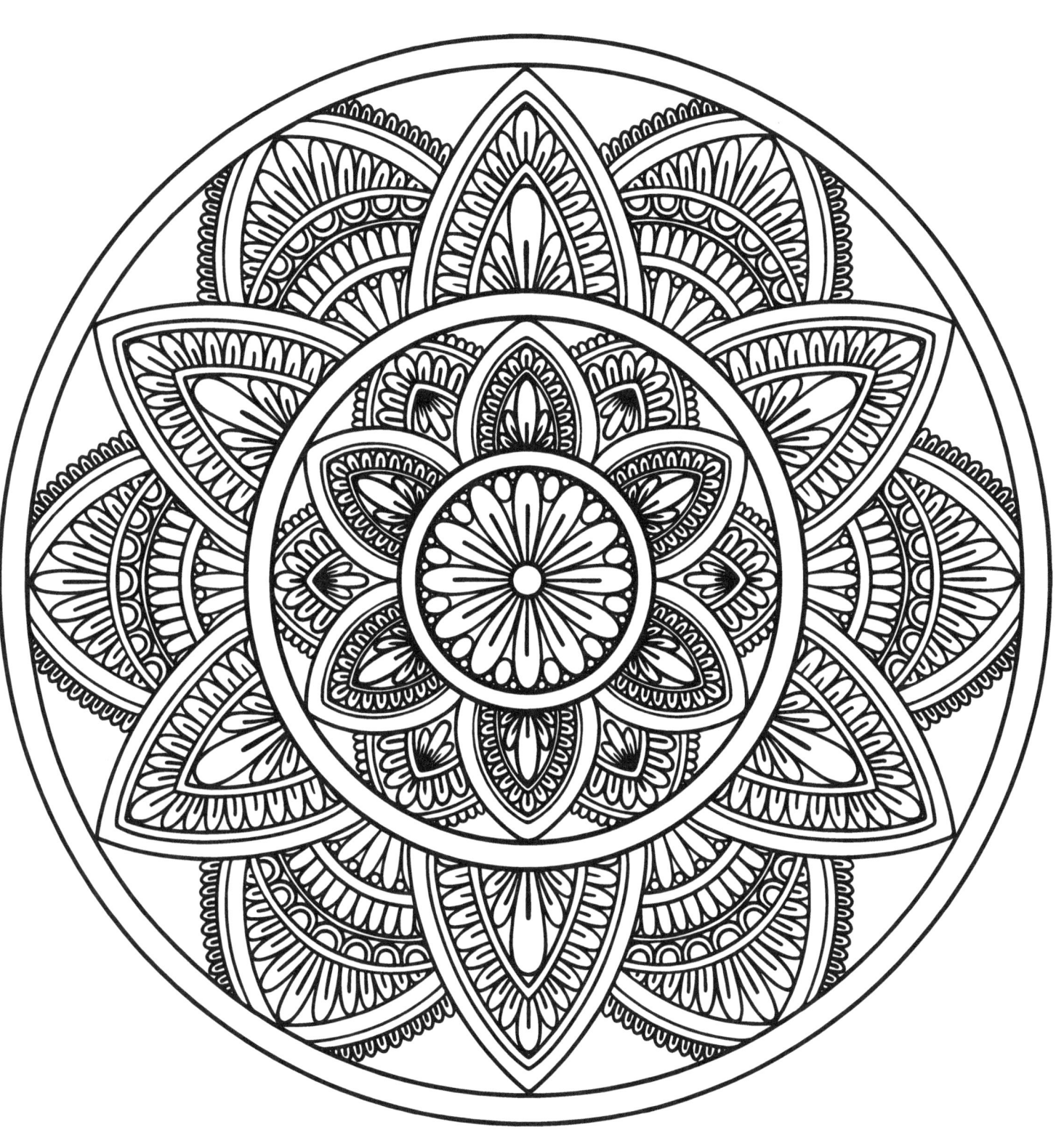

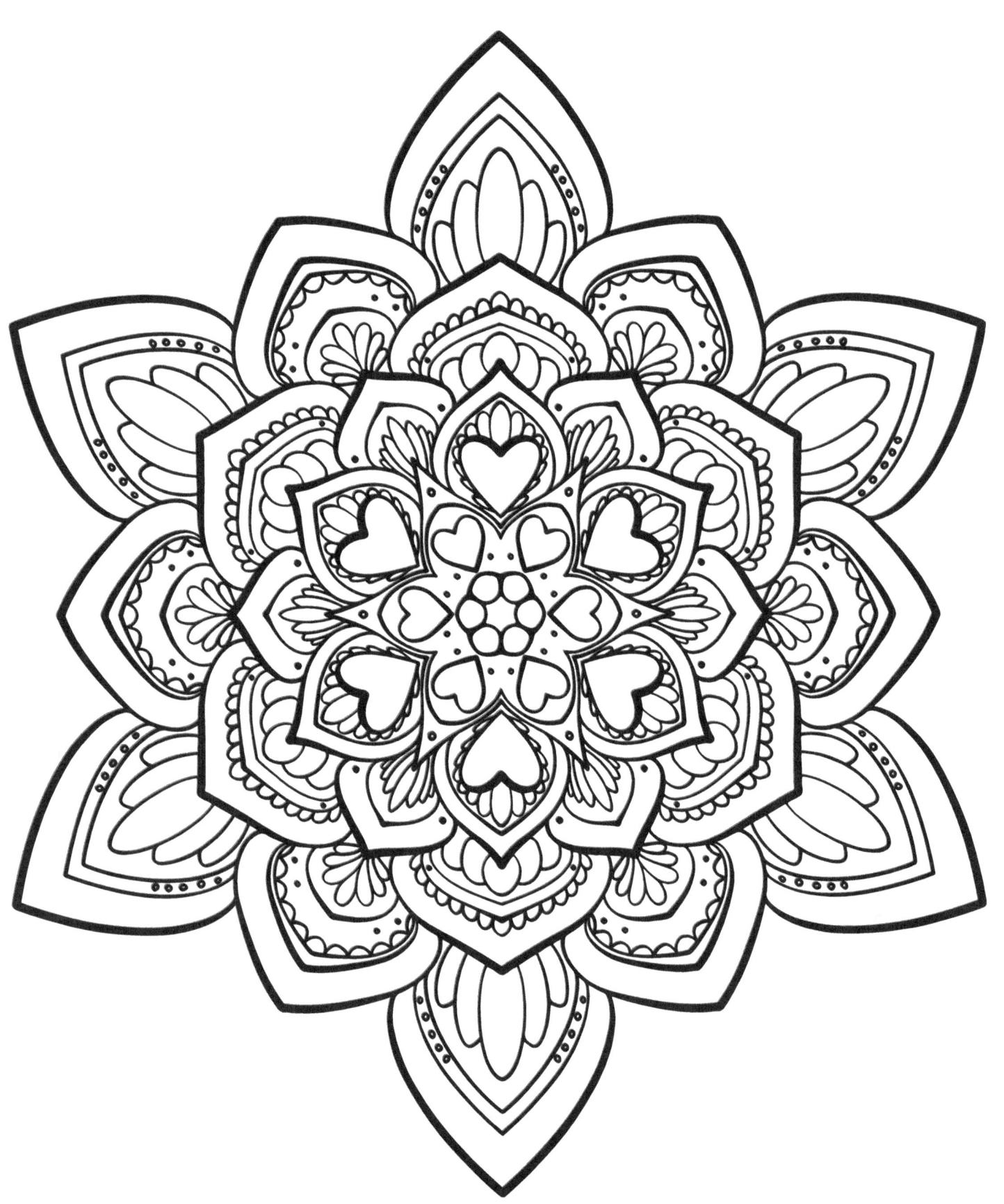

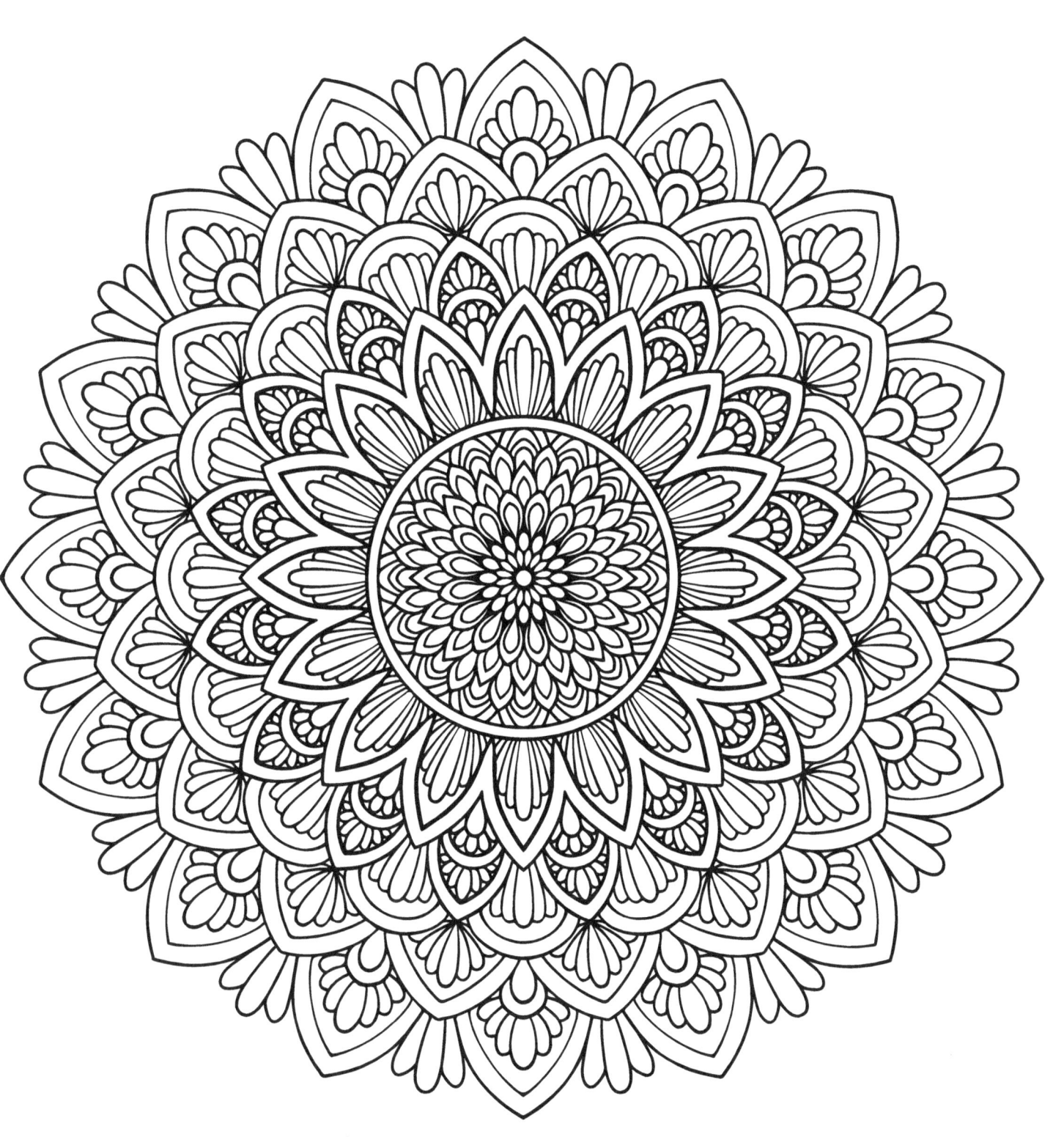

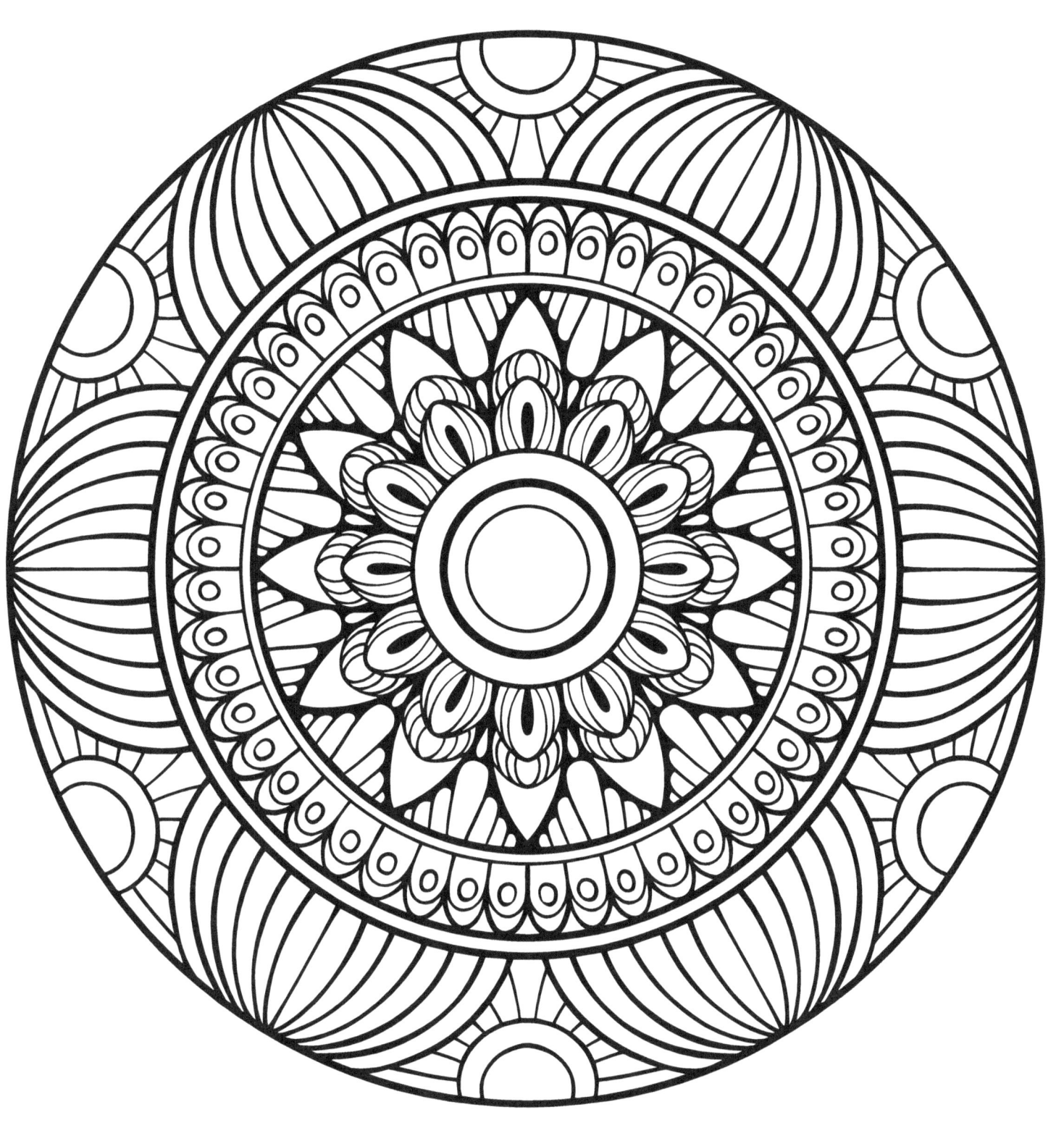

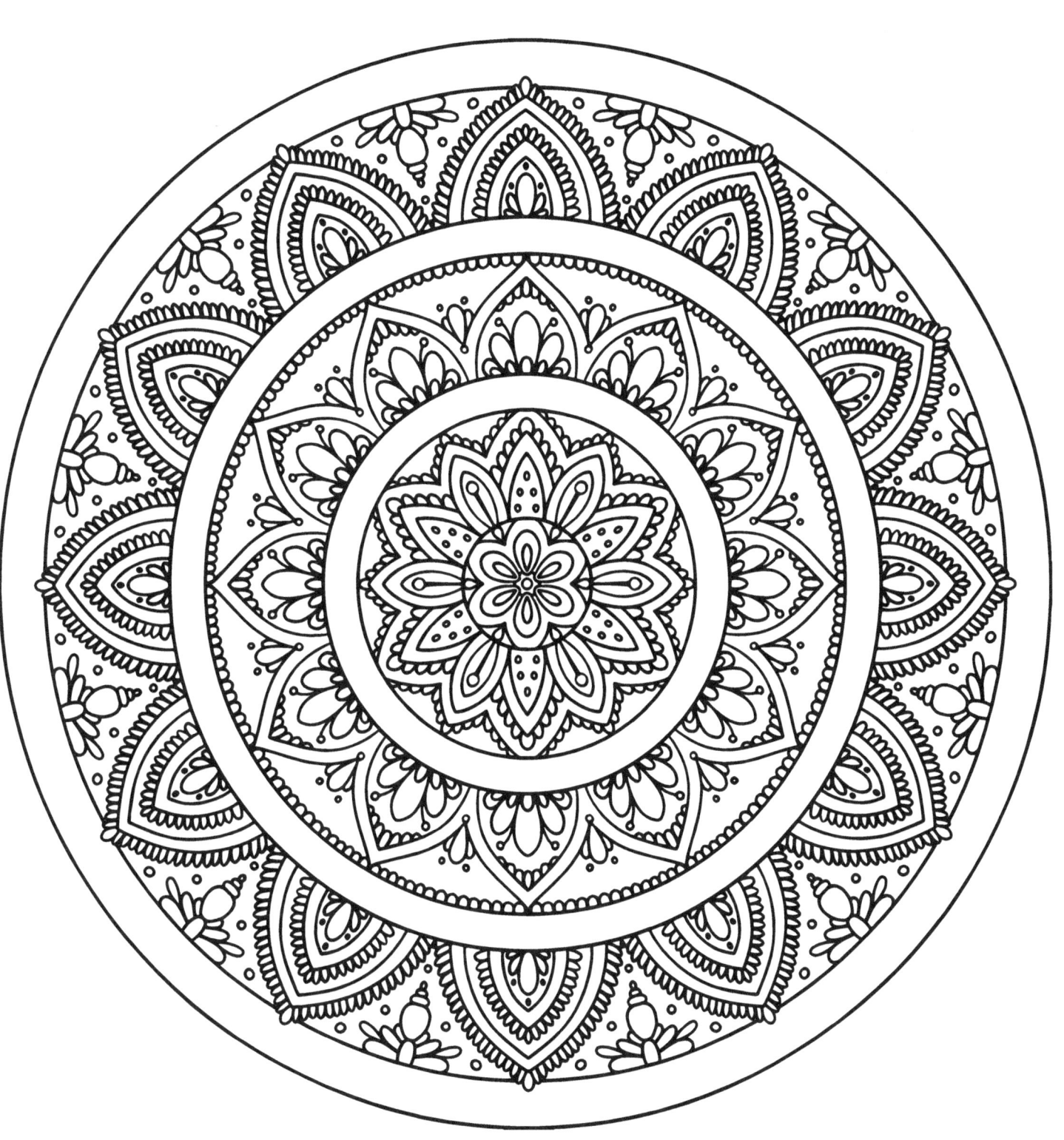

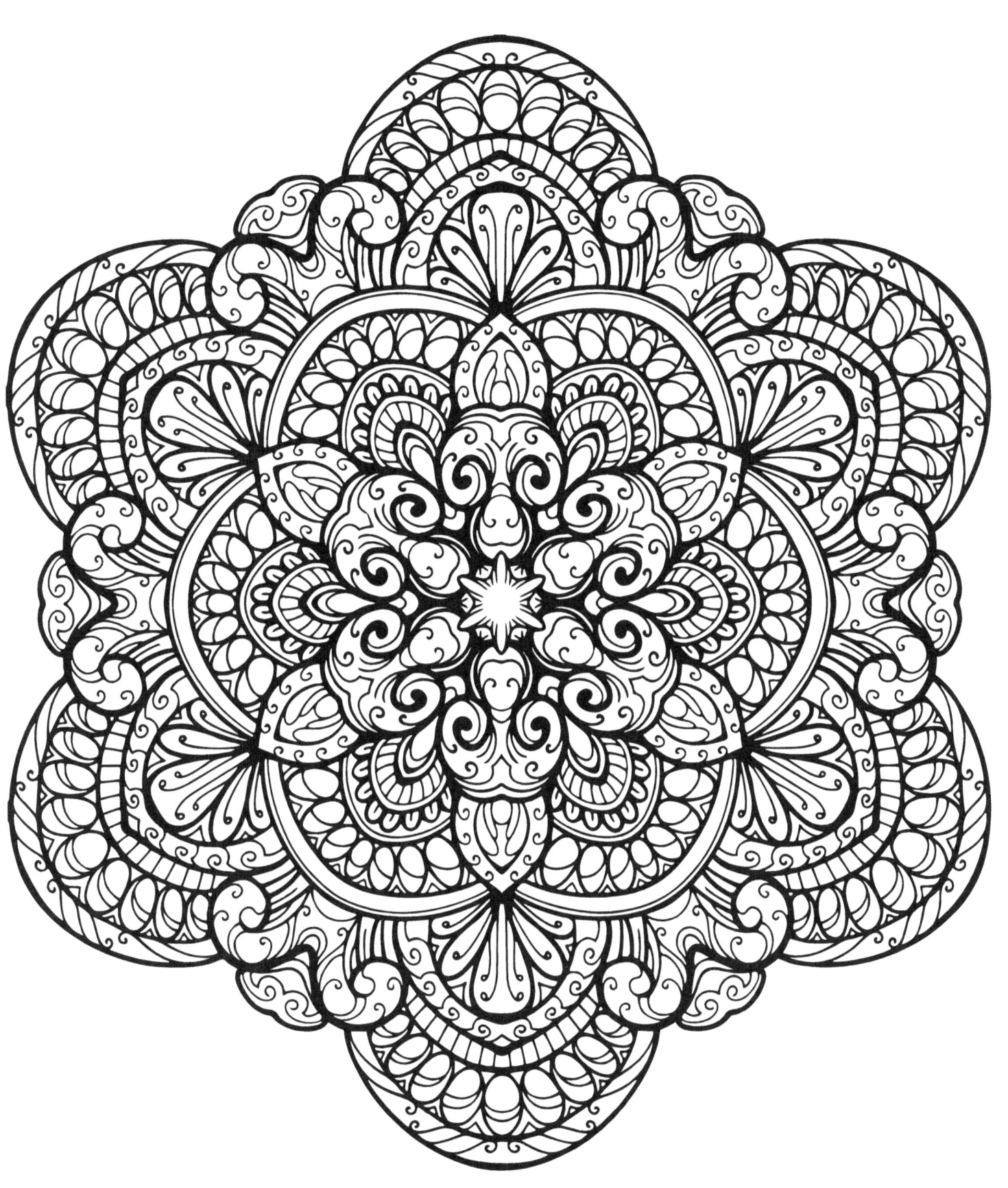

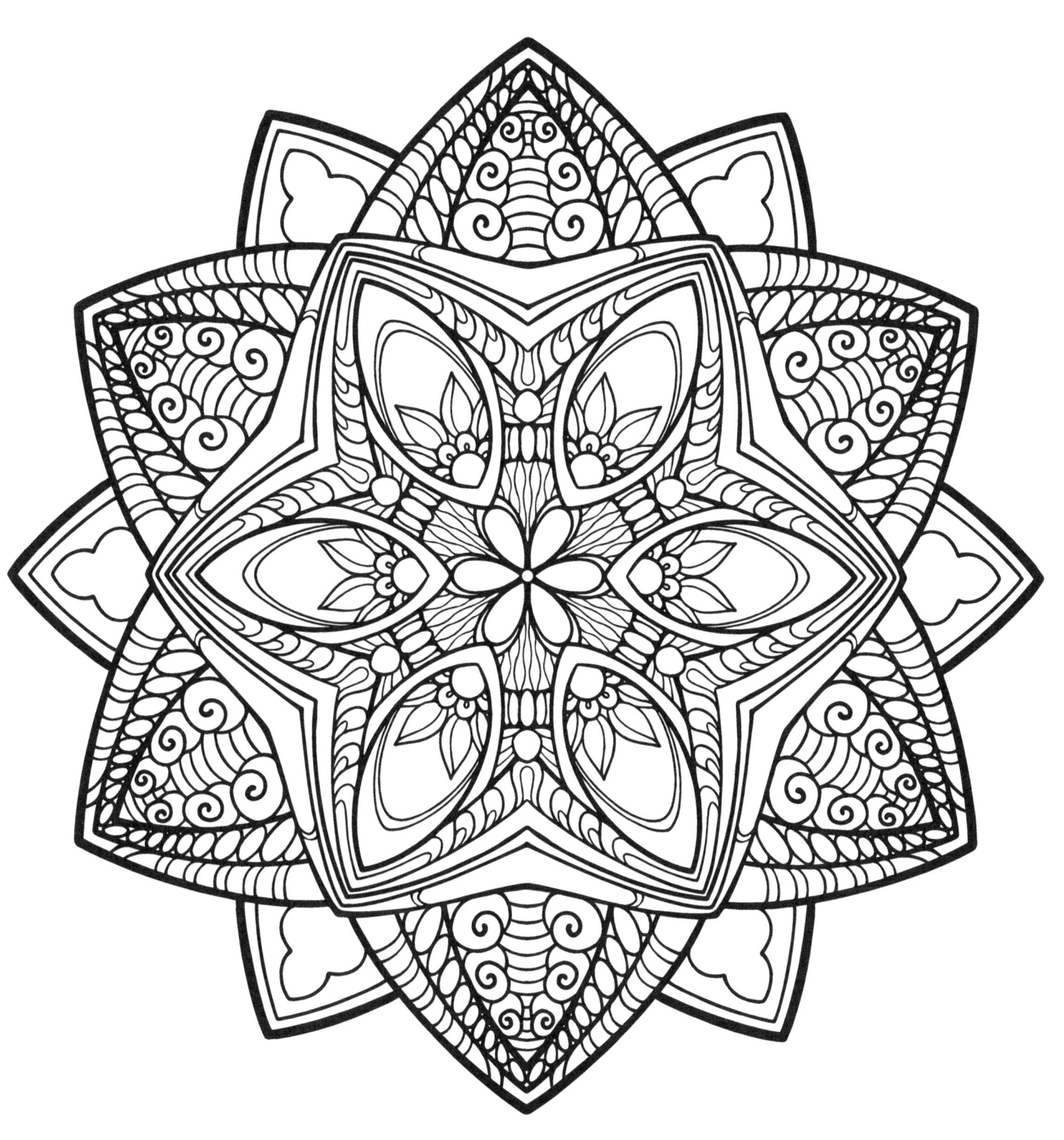

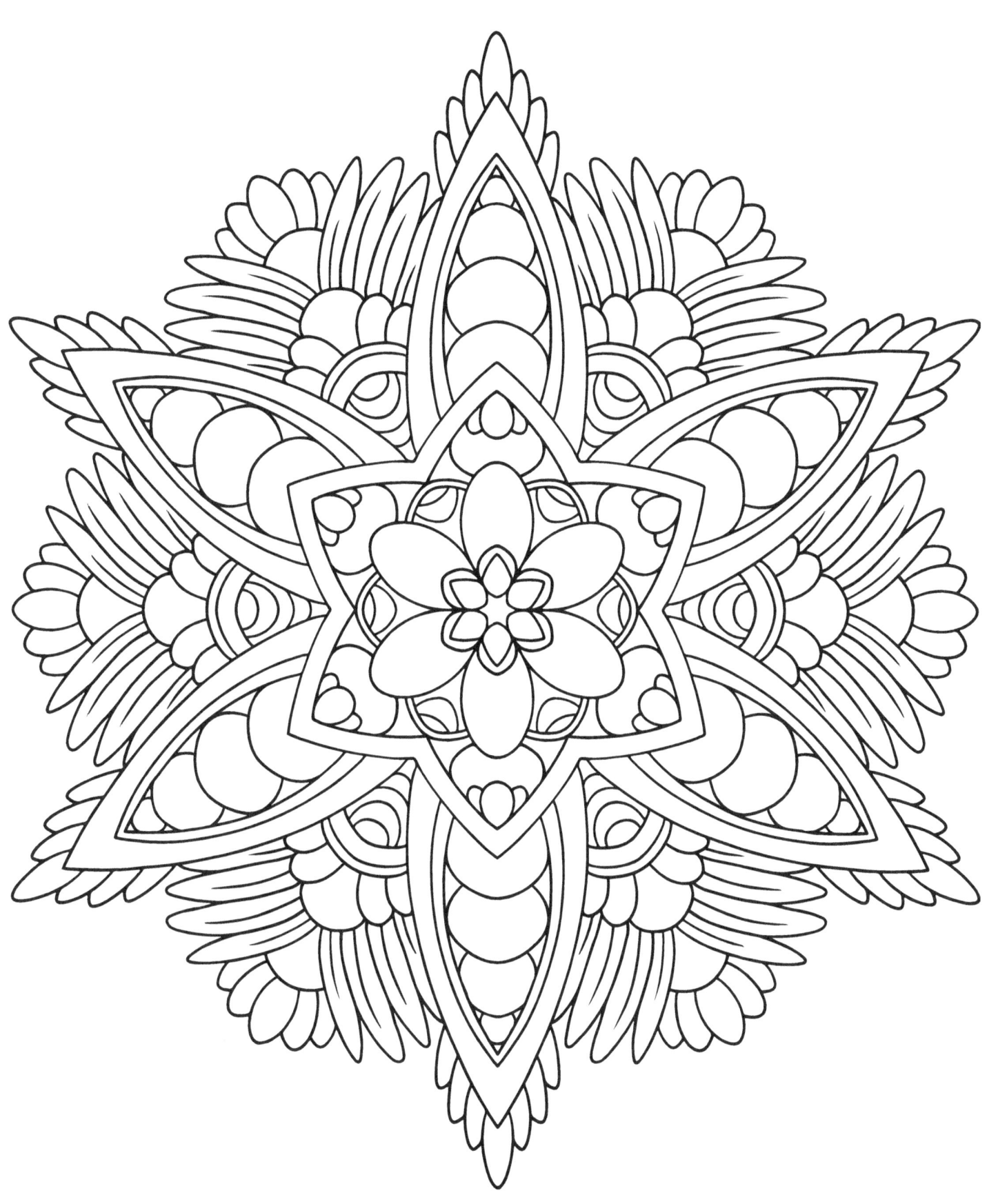

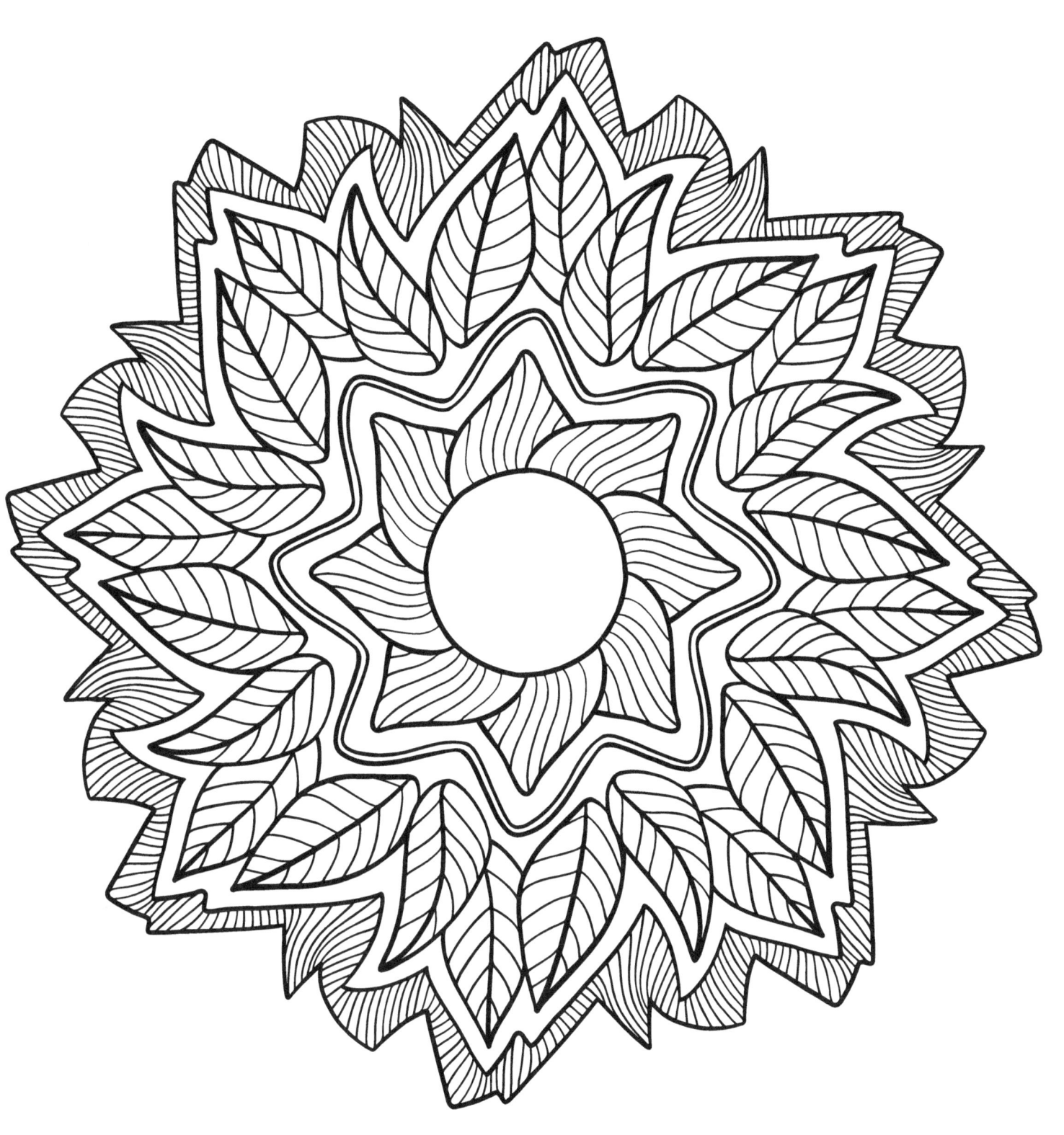

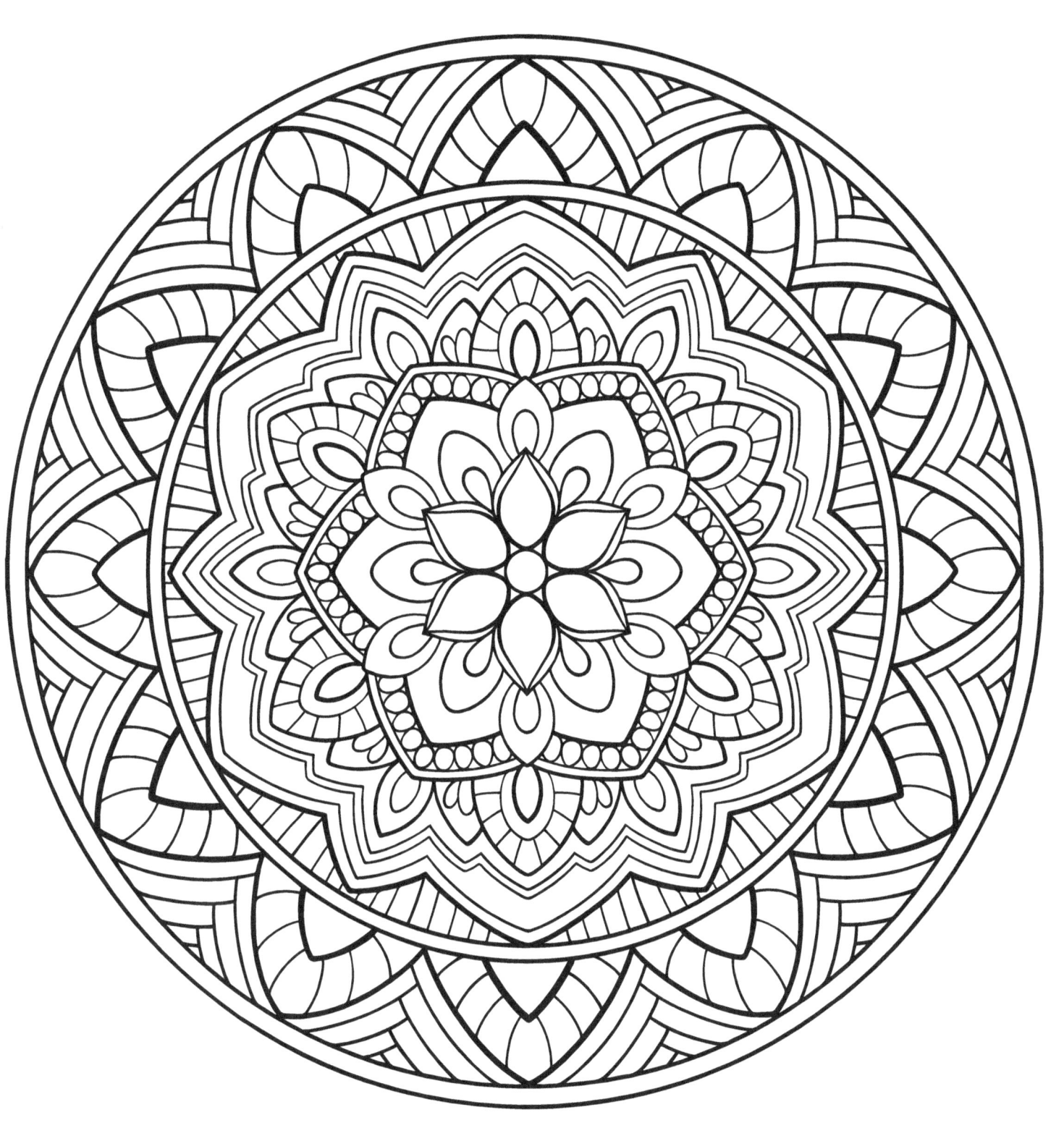

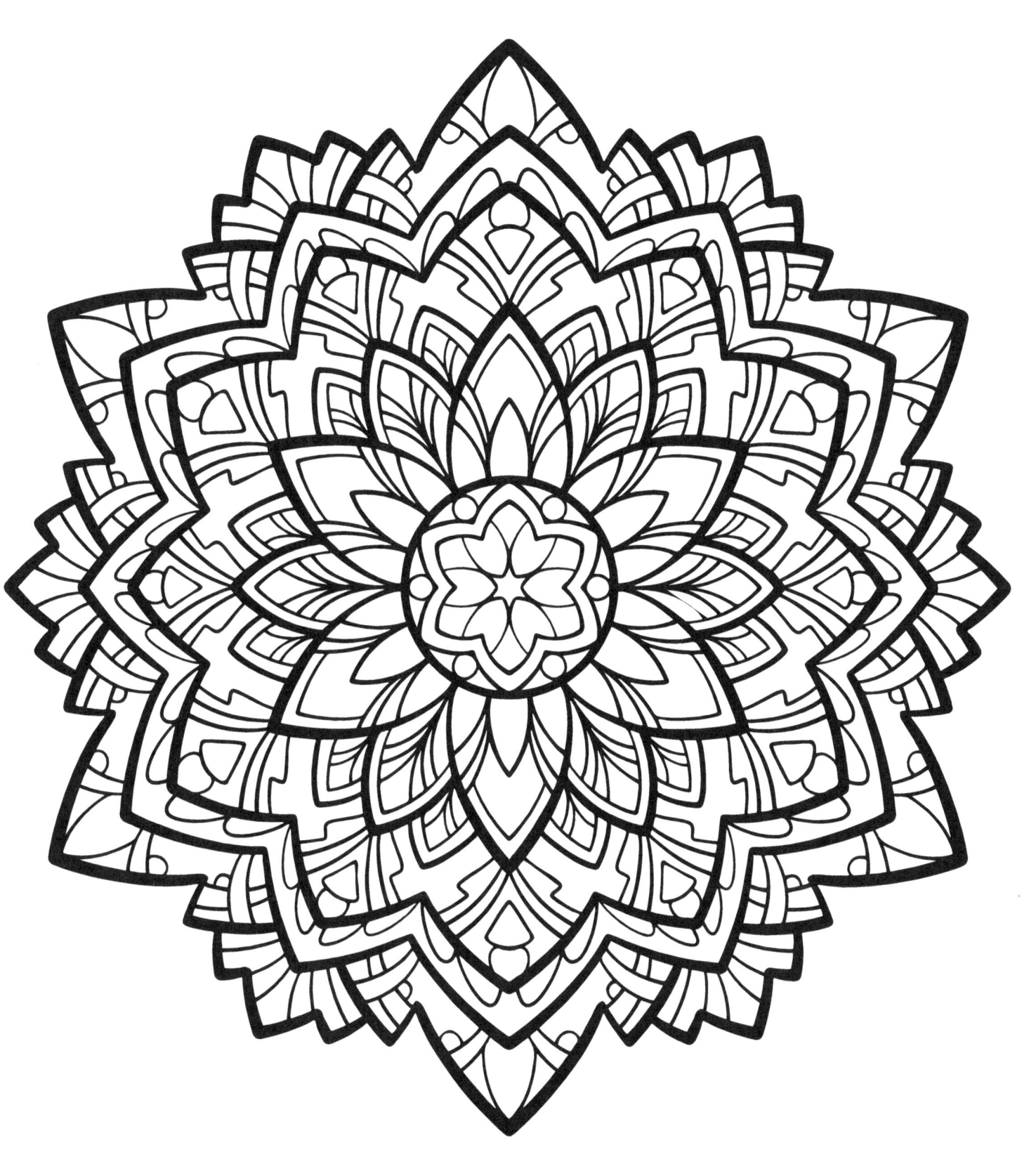

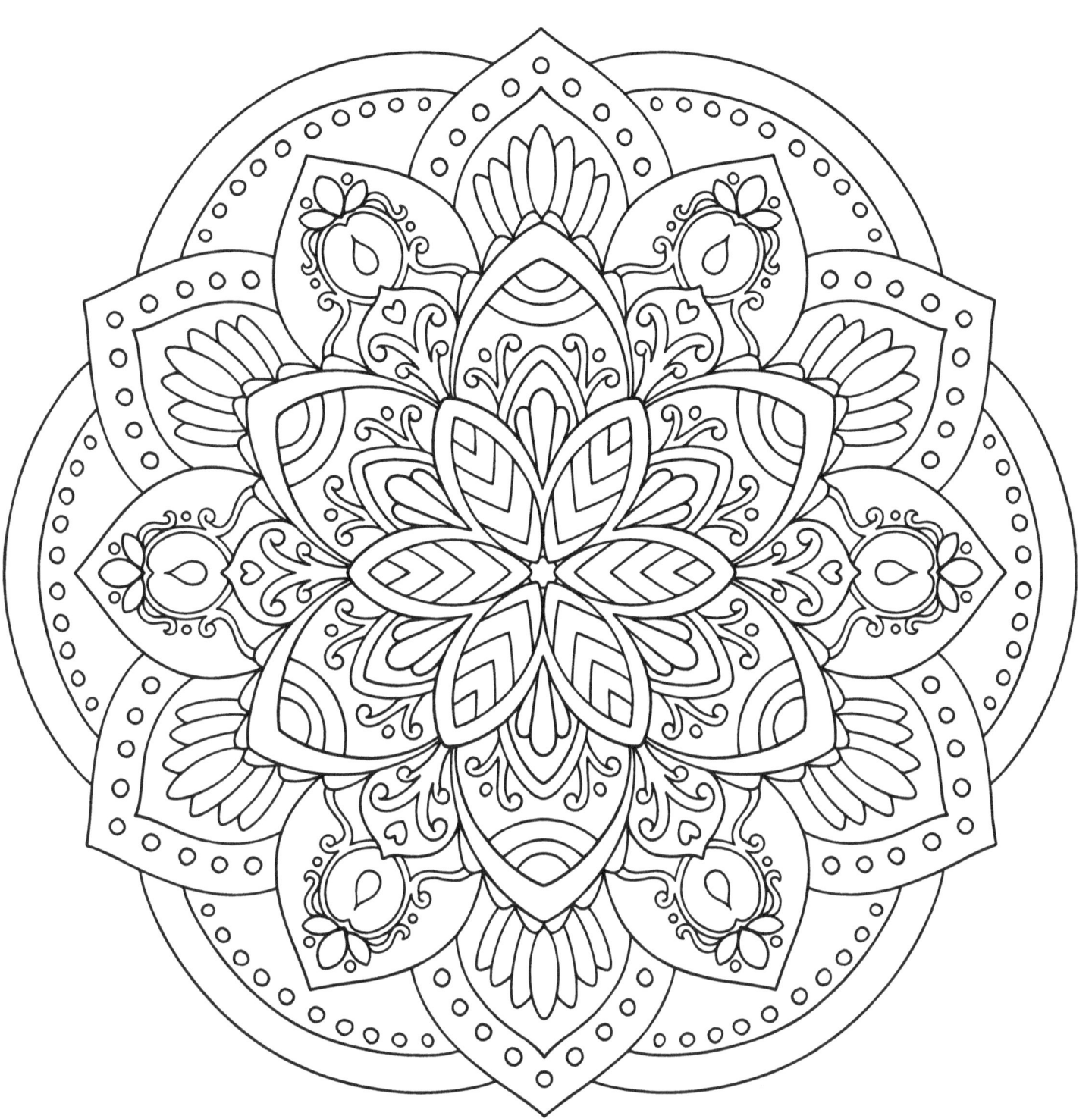

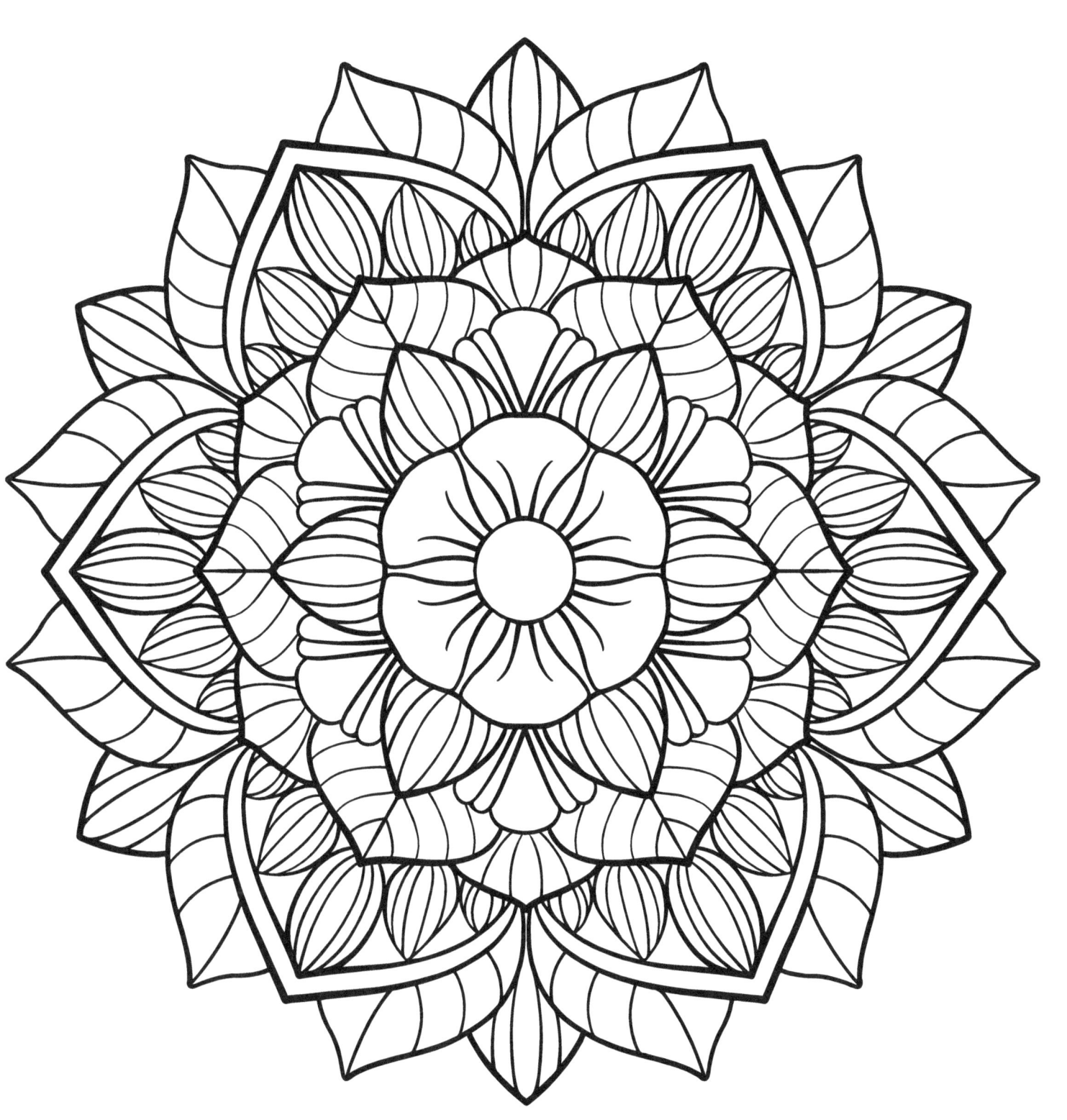

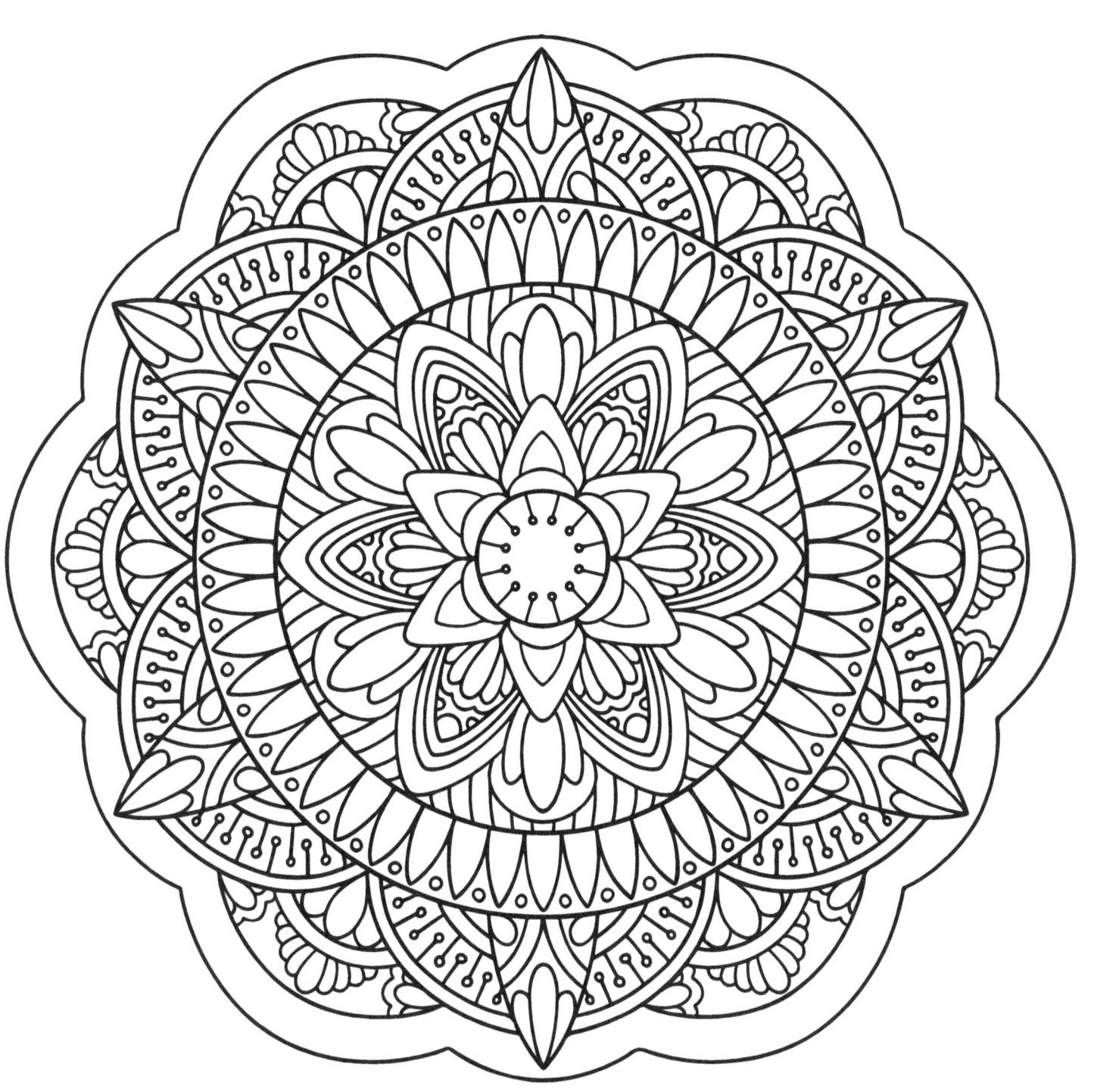

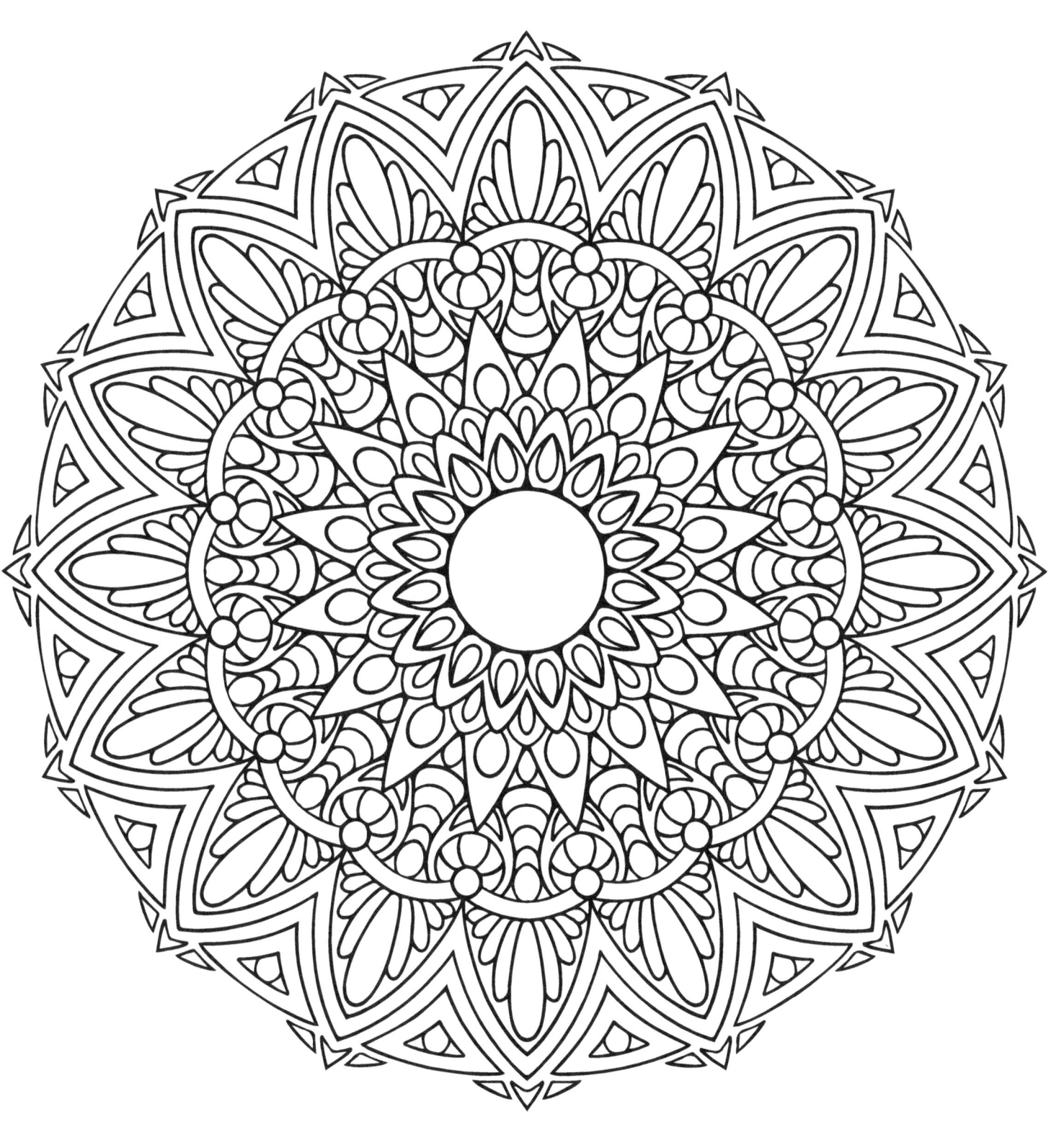

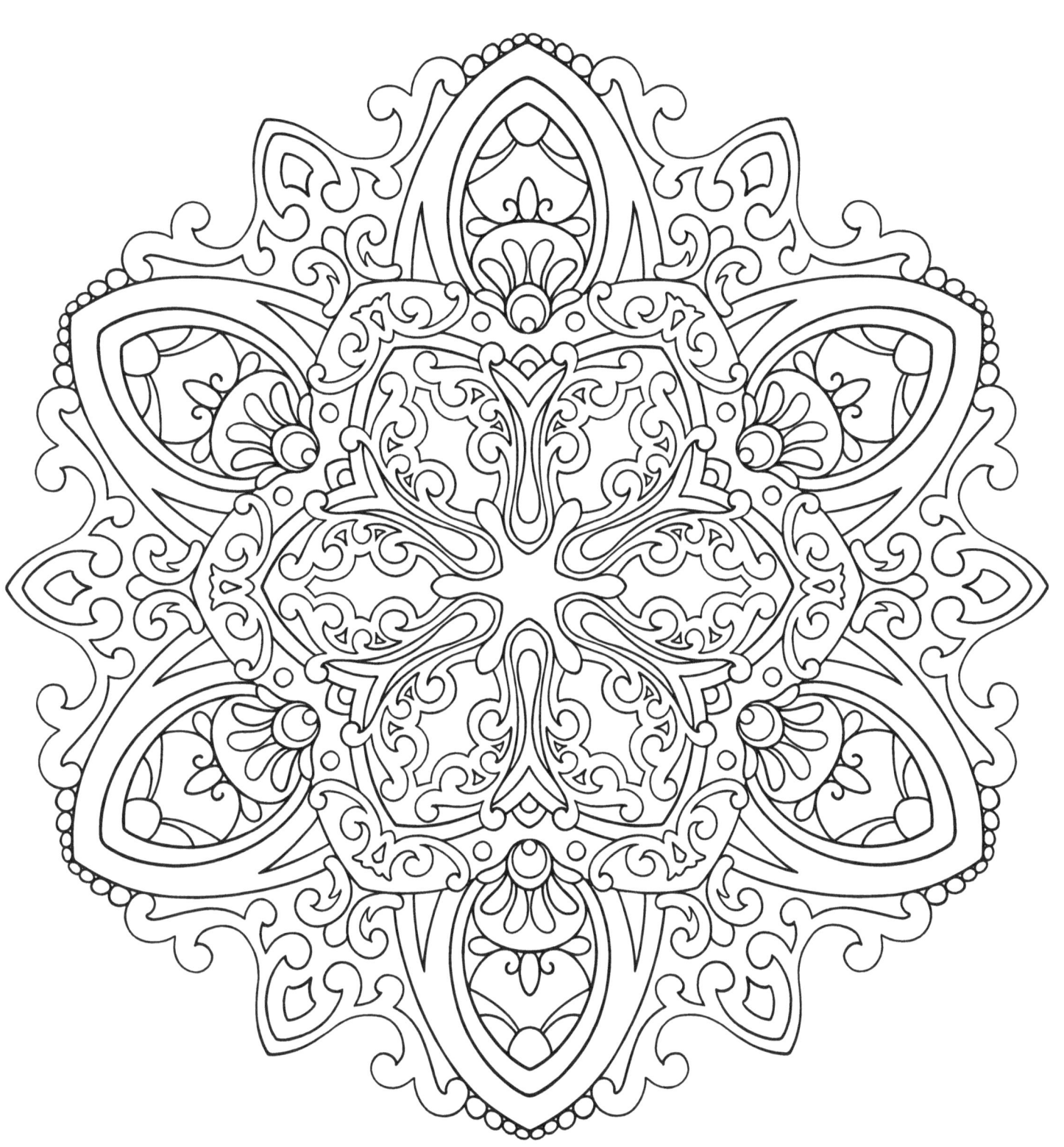

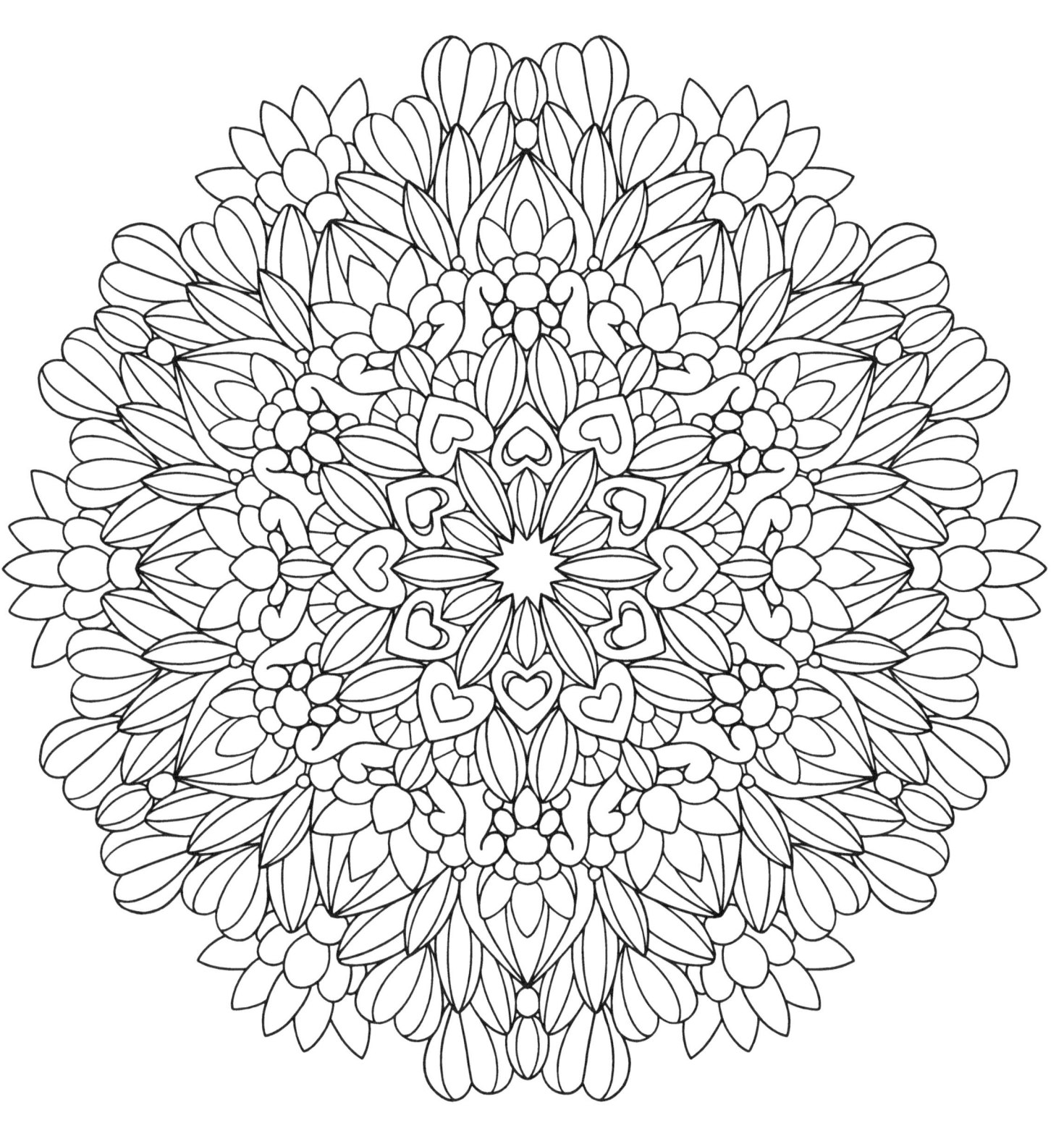

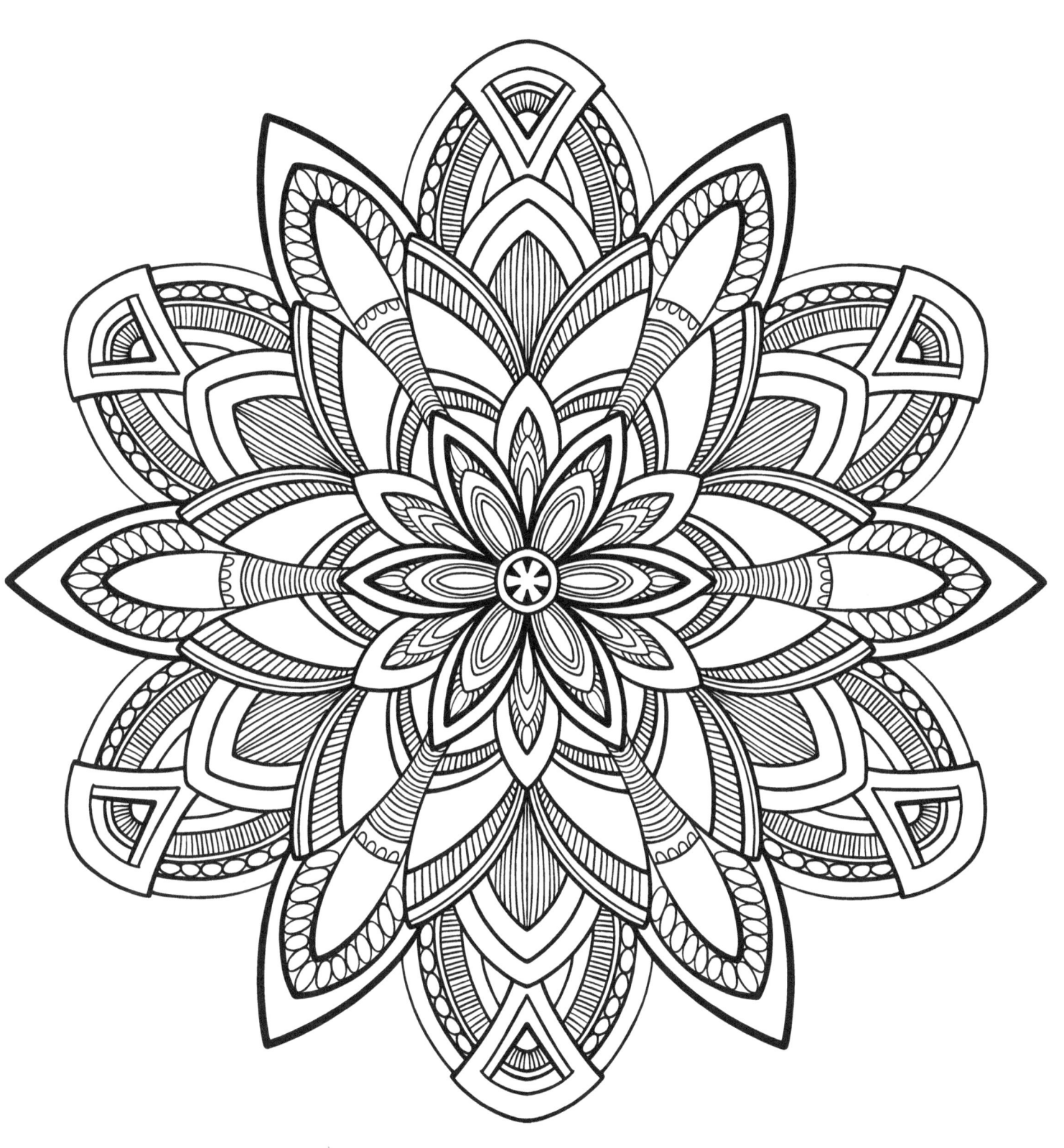

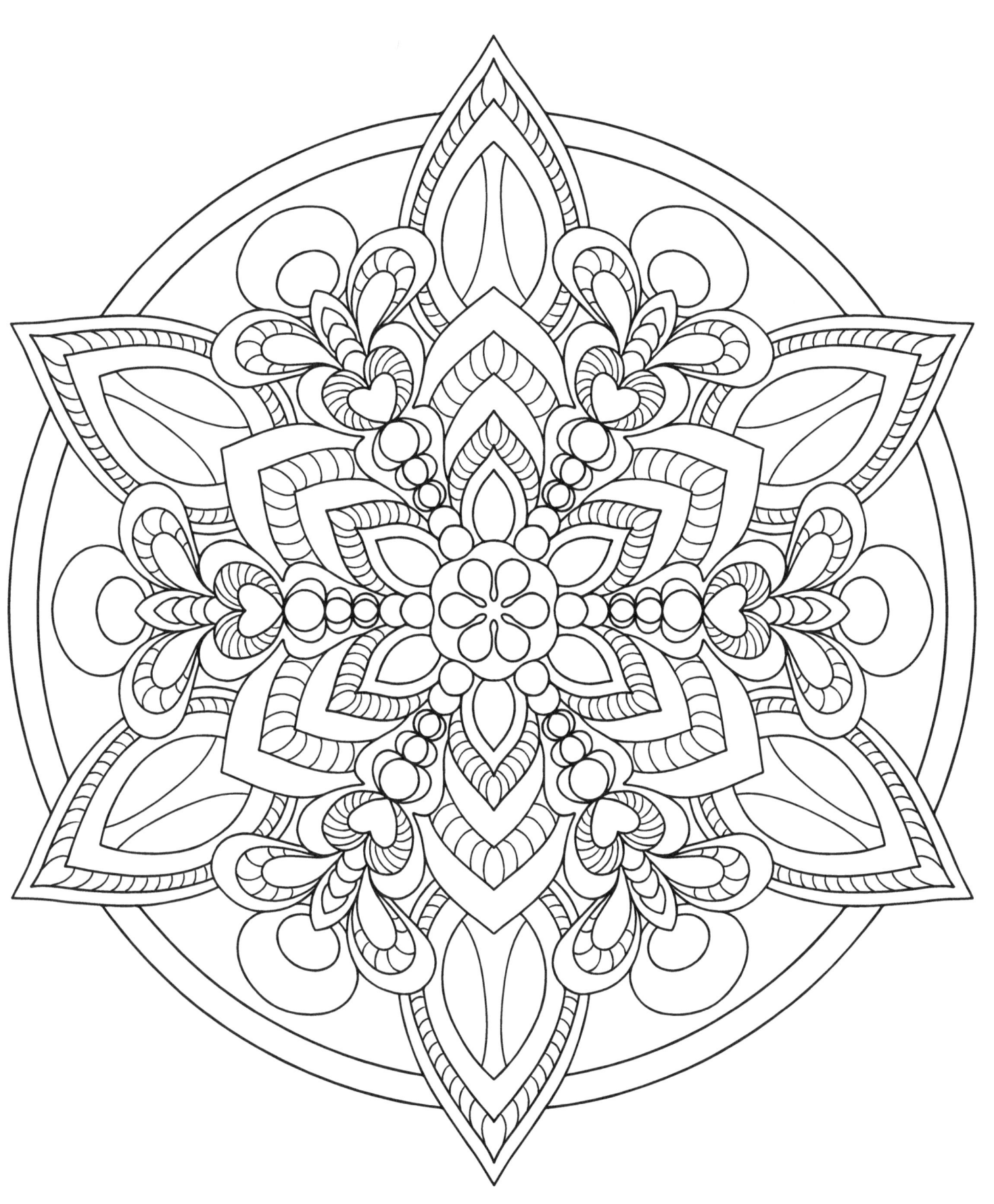

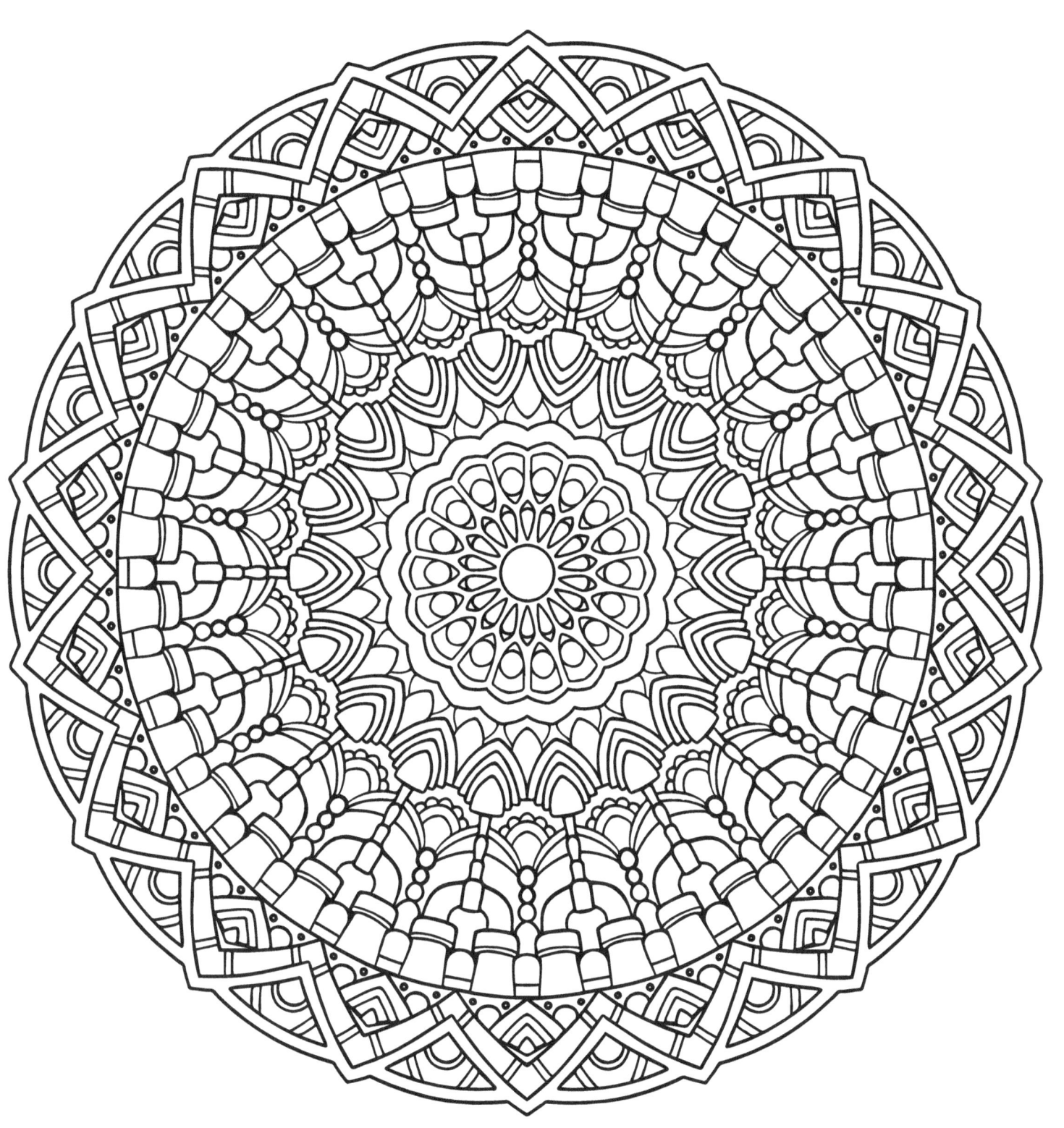

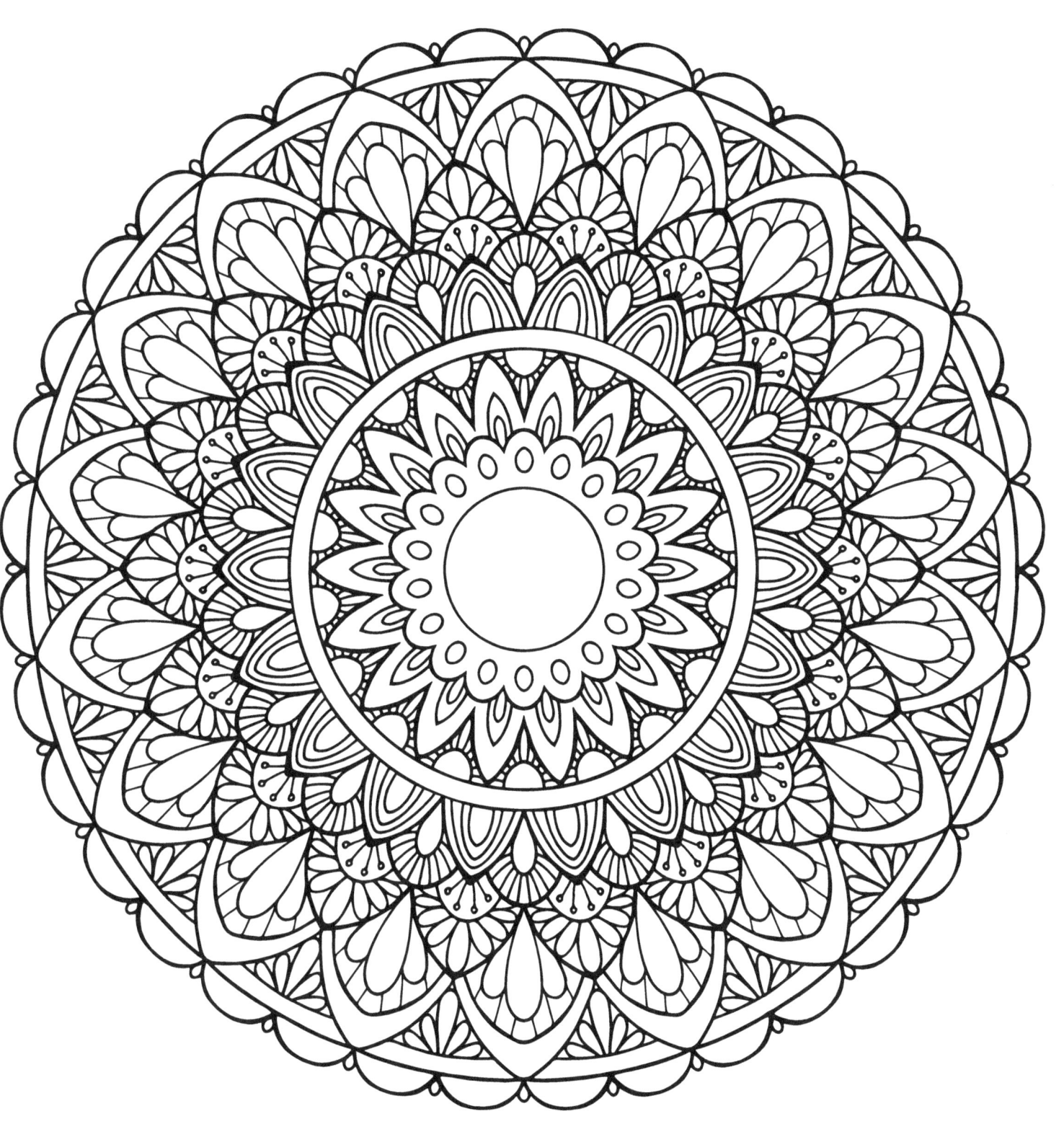

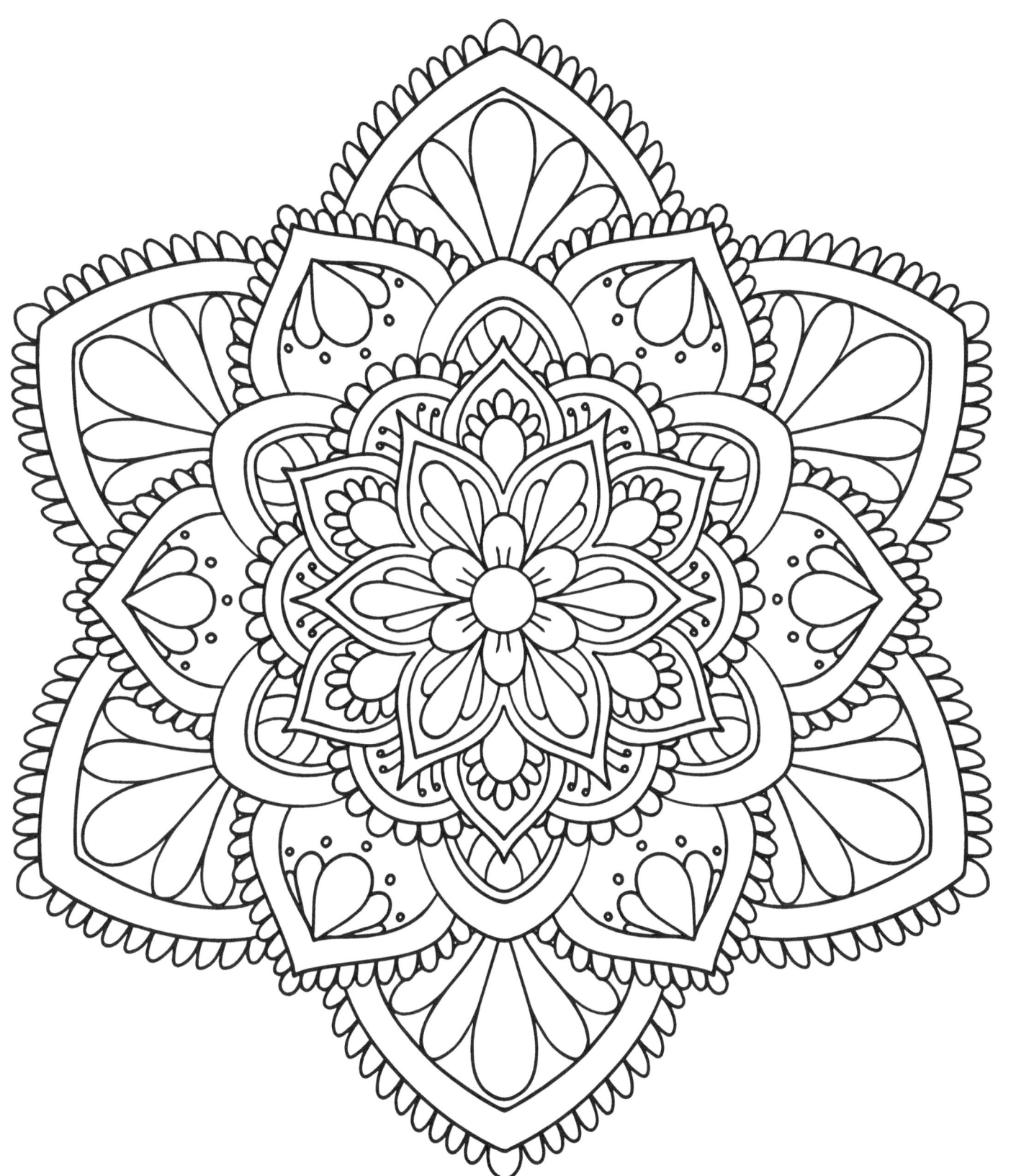

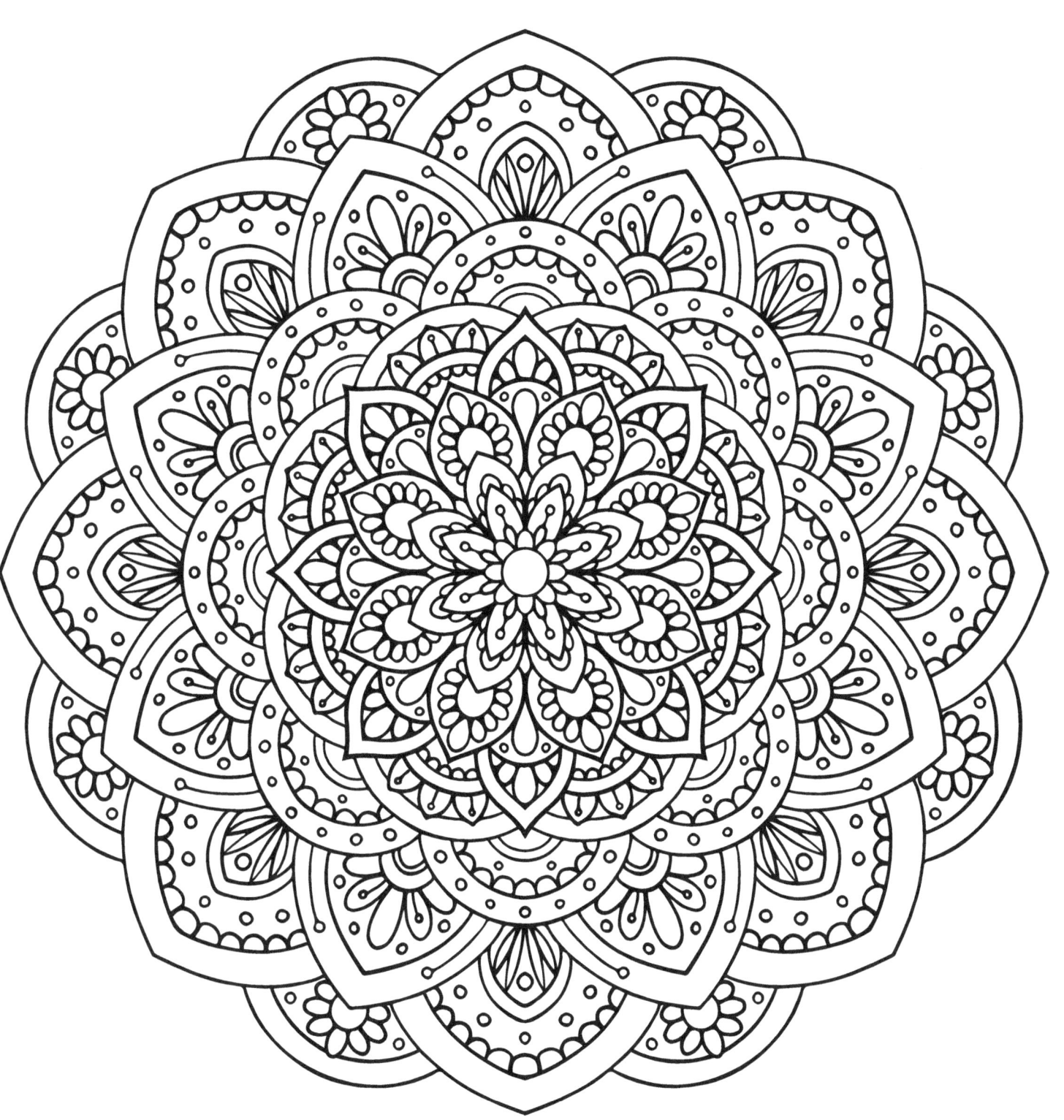

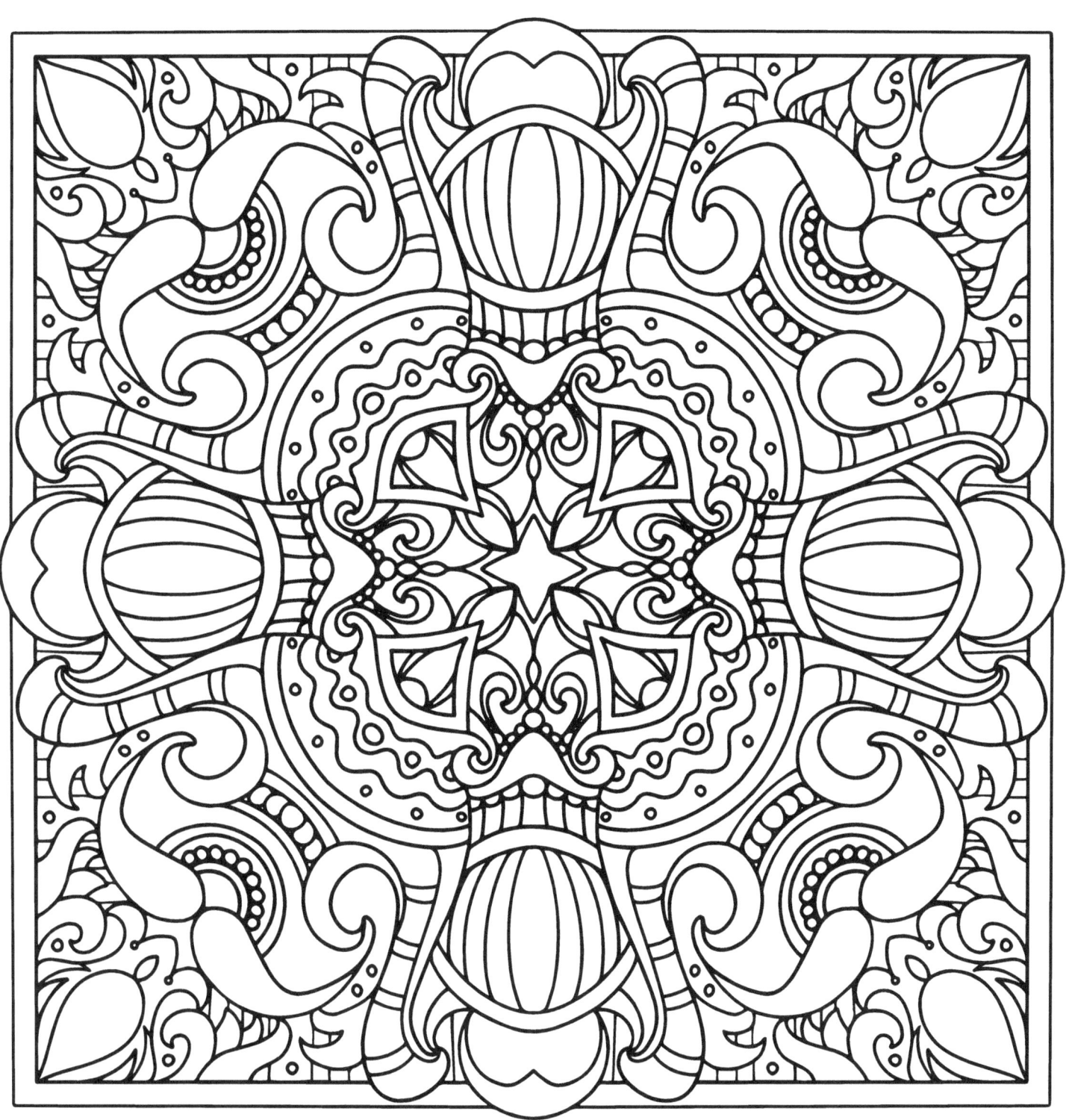

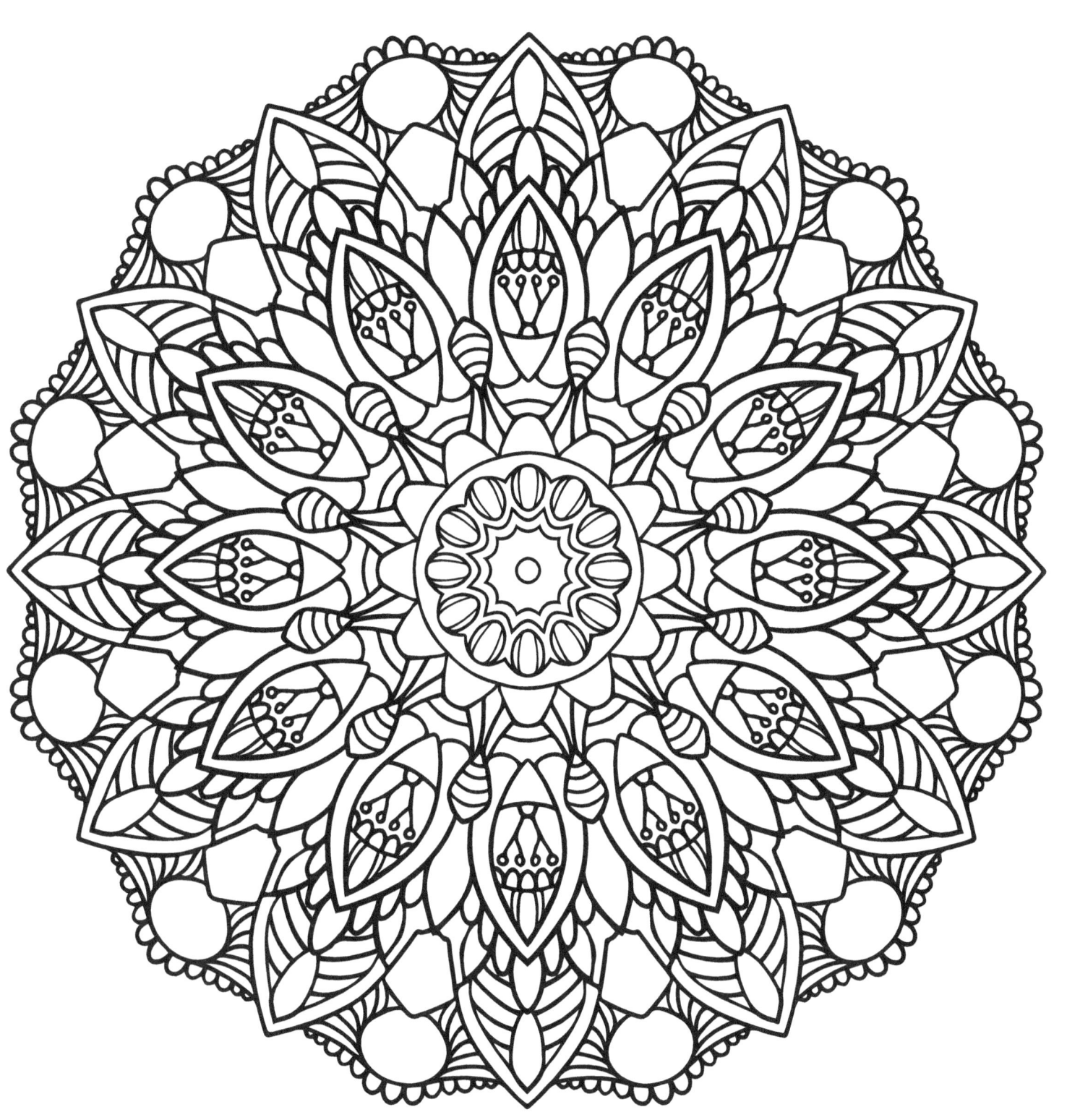

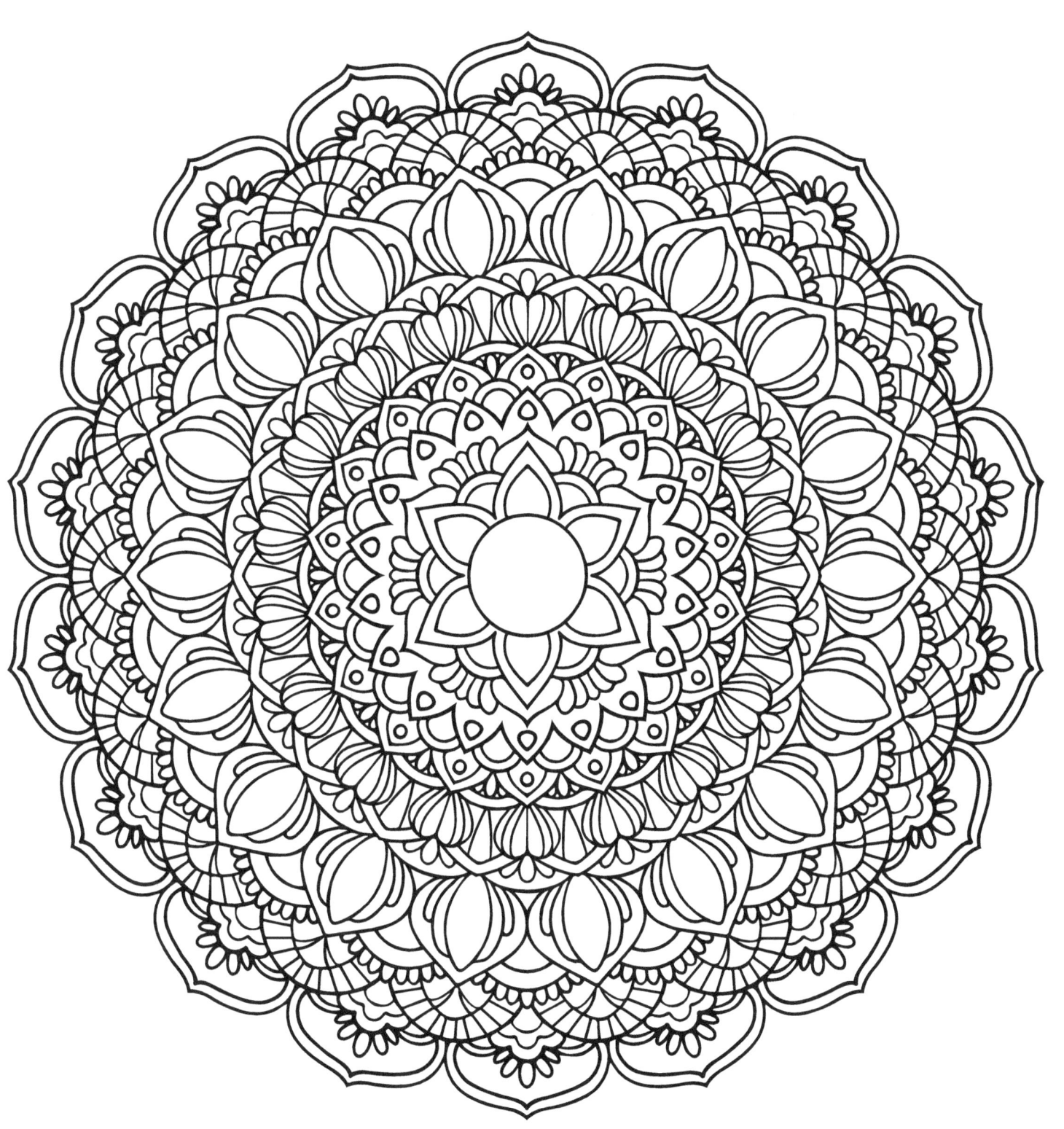

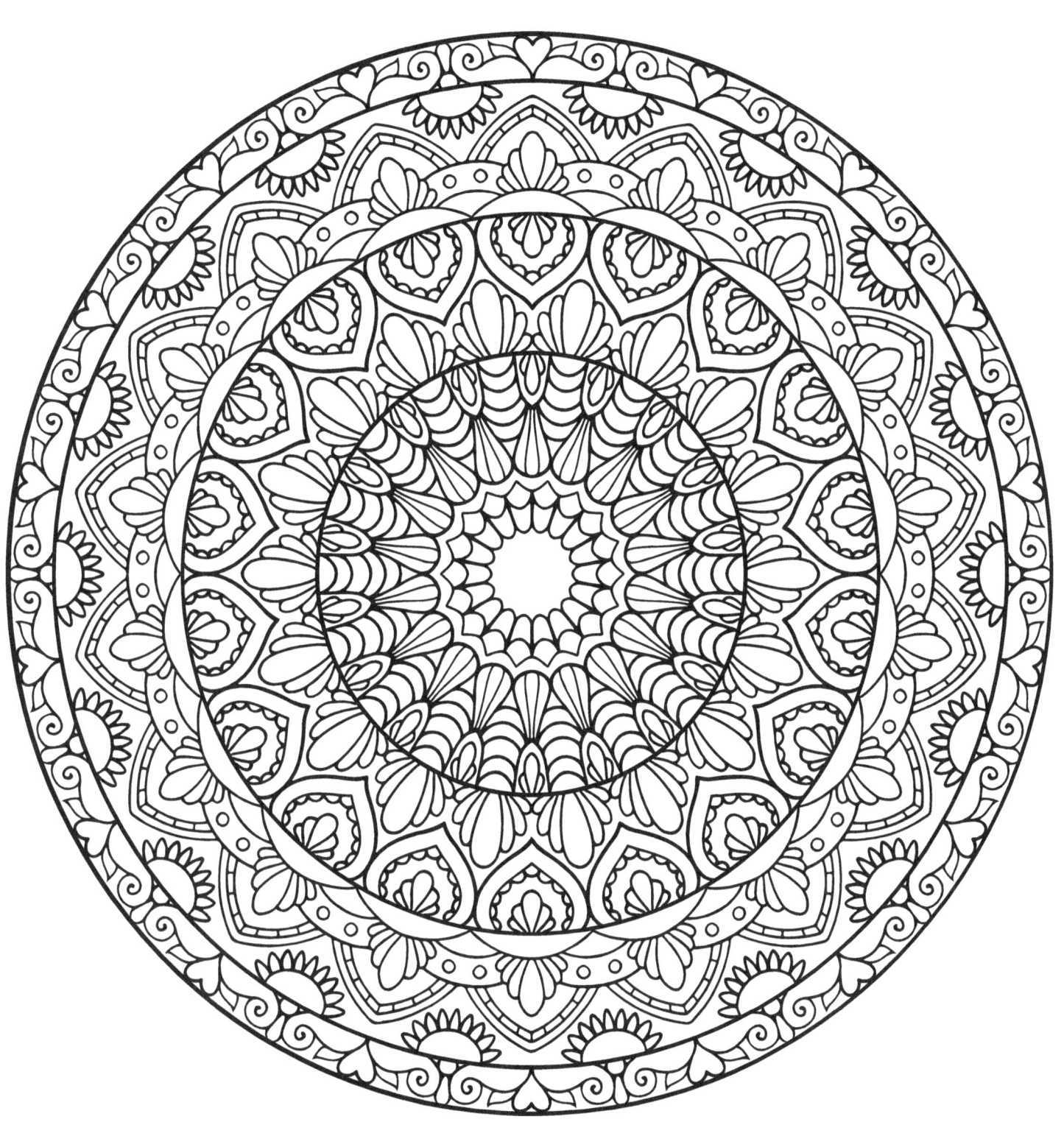

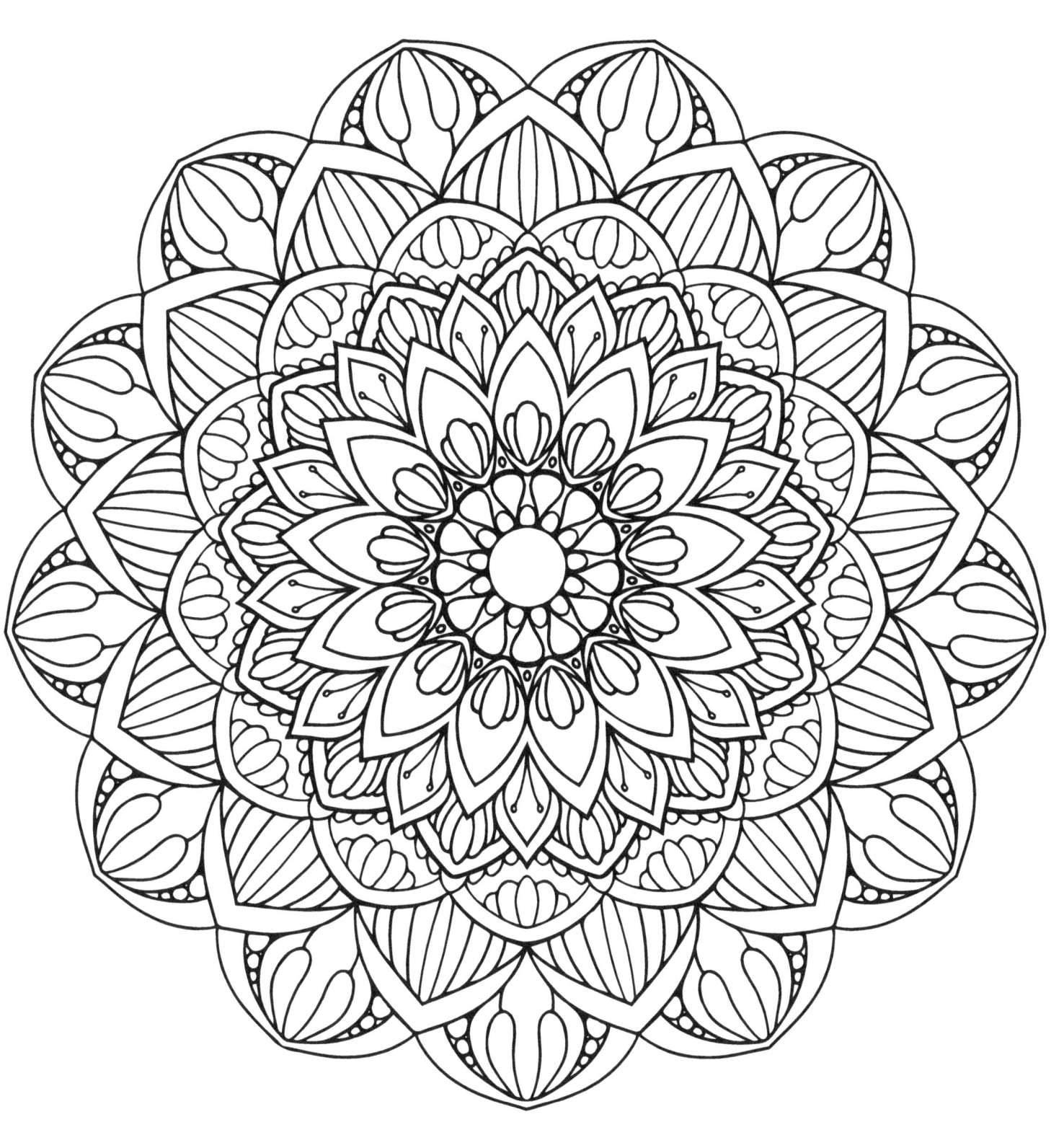

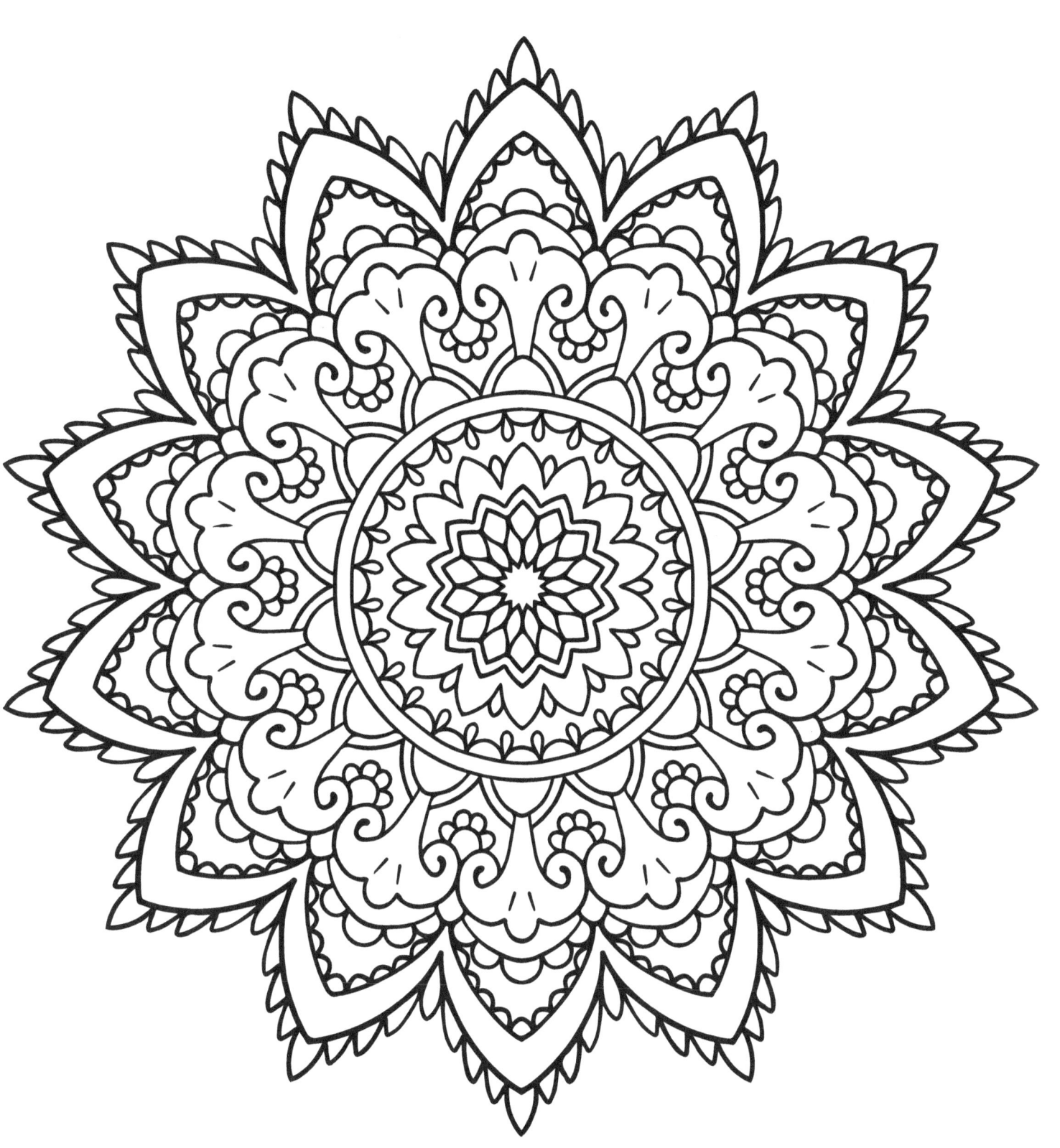

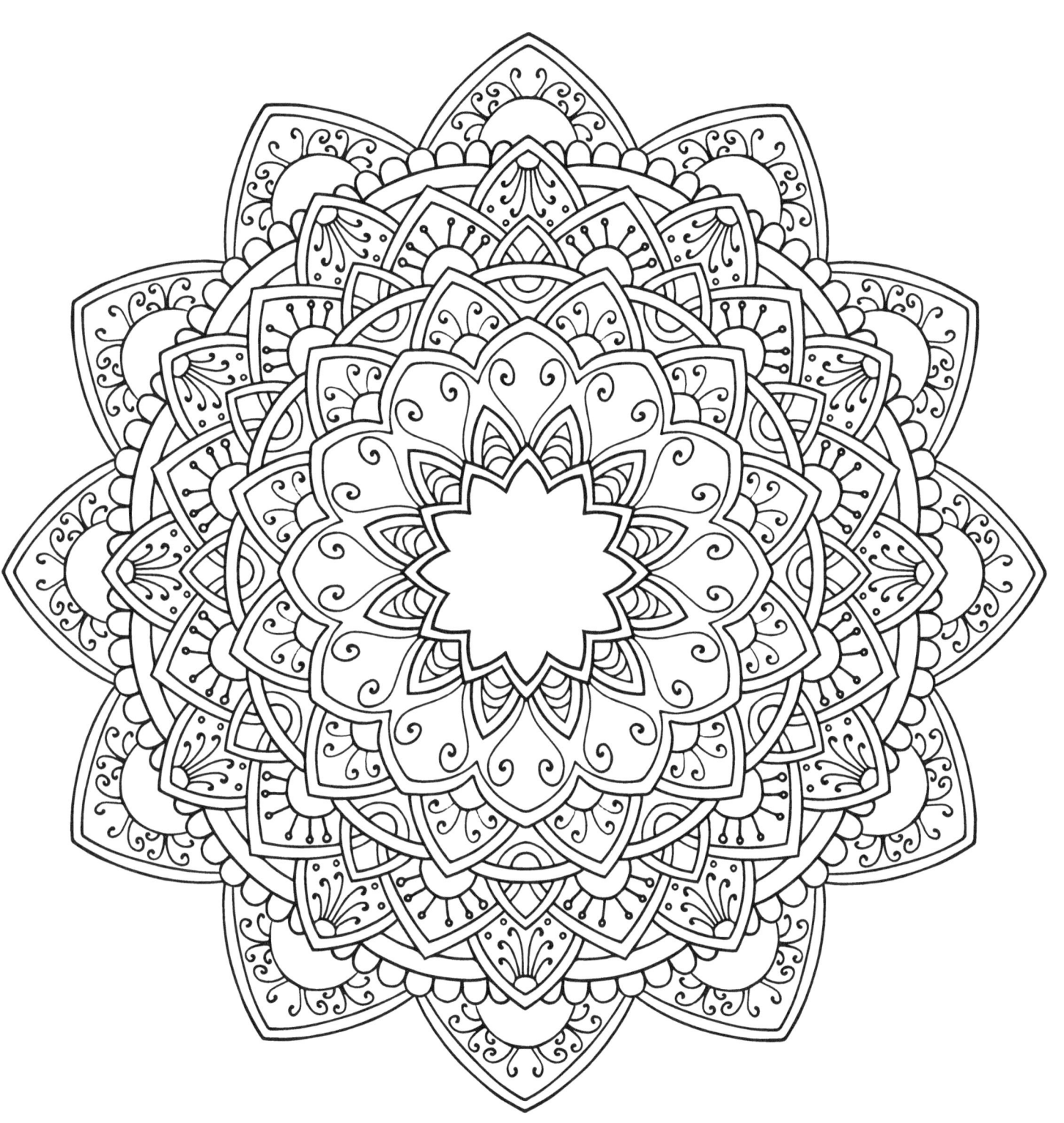

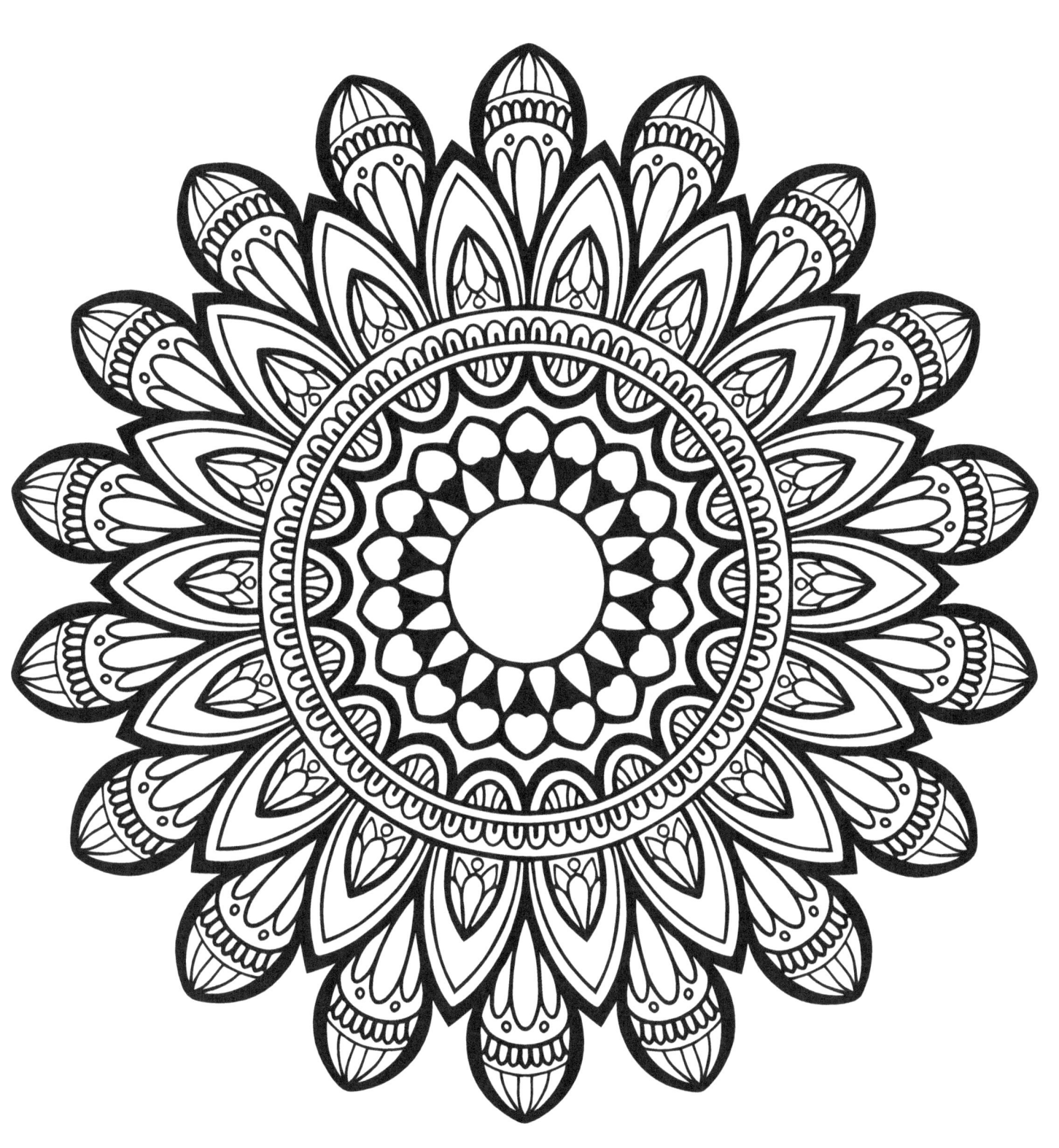

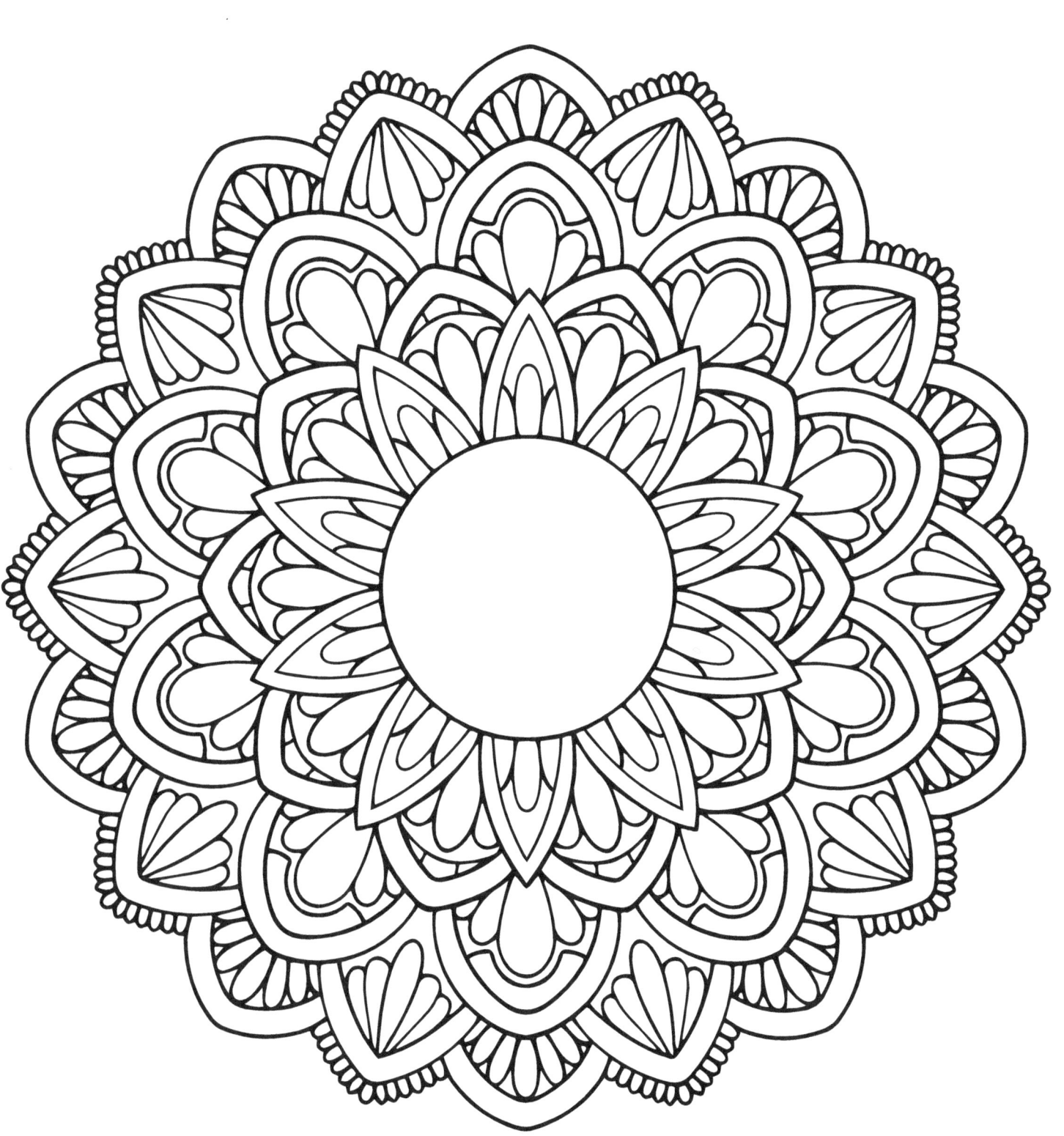

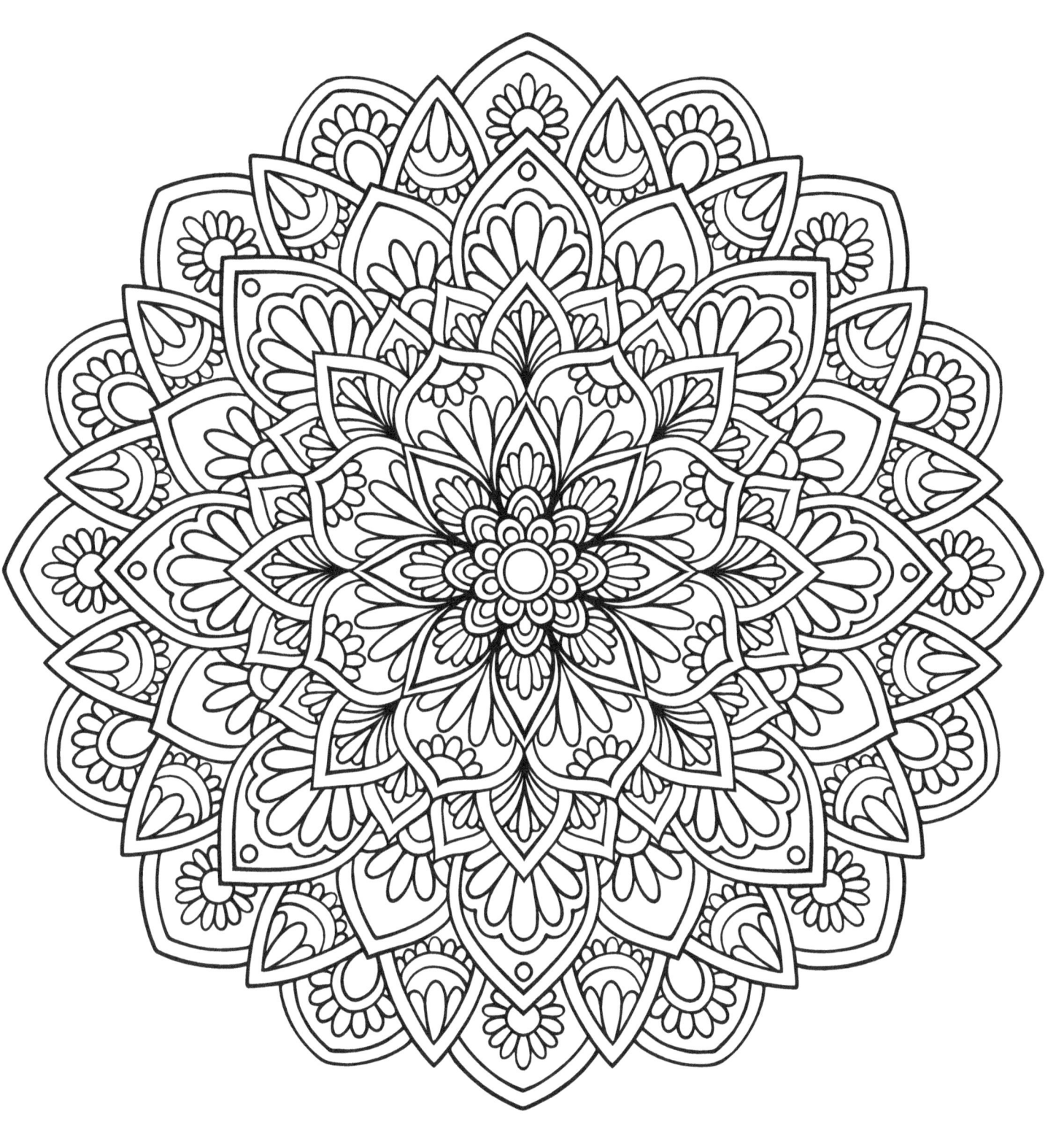

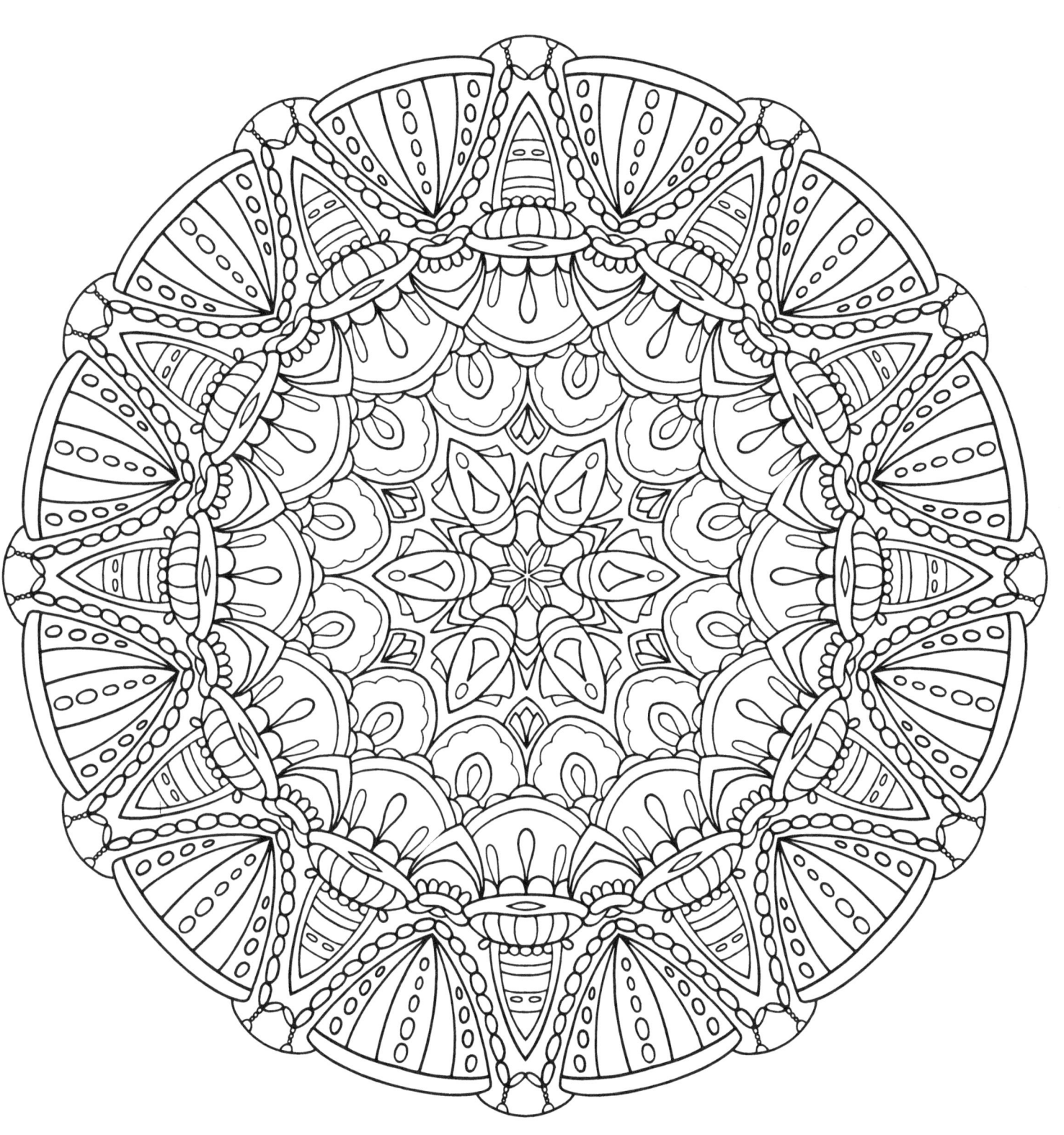

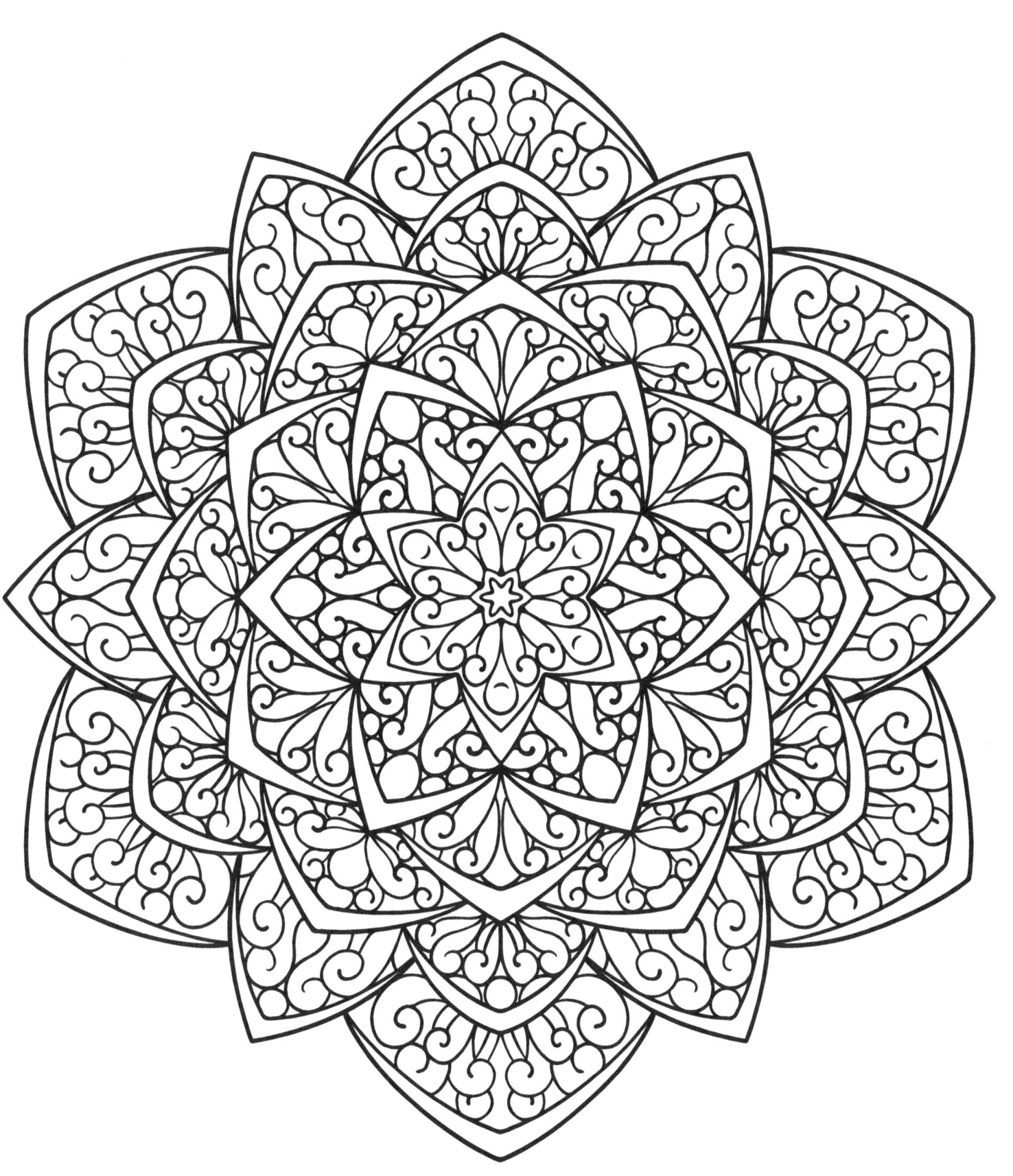

www.ingramcontent.com/pod-product-compliance
Lightning Source LLC
Chambersburg PA
CBHW081433220526
45466CB00008B/2369